A SKY WITHOUT EAGLES

JACK DONOVAN

Selected Essays and Speeches

2010 – 2014

DISSONANT HUM

CASCADIA

First Paperback Edition.

ISBN-10: 098545234X
ISBN-13: 978-0-9854523-4-6

Cover and Interior Artwork and Design by Jack Donovan.

Published by Jack Donovan.

[DH]

[DISSONANT HUM]
4230 SE King Road, No. 185
Milwaukie, Oregon. 97222
USA.

www.dissonant-hum.com

Subjects:
1. Social Sciences - Men's Studies
2. Psychology - Men
4. Men - Social Conditions
5. Sex Role
6. Gender Studies
7. Philosophy
8. Politics - Fascism
9. Politics - Anarchism

CONTENTS

★ ★ ★

PREFACE

This collection of essays and speeches is for readers who have enjoyed my work already, and who have asked for hard copies of some favorites for their own bookshelves. That's why I'm releasing it first in hardcover, my first stab at that format.

It begins with "Violence is Golden," which may be the most popular essay I've ever written. "Violence is Golden" was originally intended to be an opening chapter for an early draft of *The Way of Men*, but I scrapped that idea and published it on *Arthur's Hall of Viking Manliness* in 2010. Since then it has been discovered and re-posted online many times, and it's often the first piece of my work that men read. This is the first time it has been available in print (or audiobook) form.

A friend suggested that I call this book "Violence is Golden and Other Essays." That's a great title, but this volume isn't about violence. As I assembled my best online writing from the past few years, I realized that there was a consistent message. Many themes are repeated and developed, but the over-arching theme of my work for the past several years has been masculine disillusionment with "The American Dream."

When I started writing for *Alternative Right* in 2010, I was advocating for "a resurgence of masculine virtue in the West," and, specifically, in America. As my investigation of masculinity deepened and *The Way of Men* took shape, I realized that contemporary American and Western ideas and institutions were actually causes of man's decline and inseparable from it.

I grew up in Pennsylvania, surrounded by American colonial architecture and design. There were American eagles everywhere, especially after the bicentennial revival of colonial style in 1976. Proles and middle-class folks like my grandparents bought moulded plastic eagles and you'd see them over doors and entranceways, like pagan symbols of good luck. I have a few of them in my living room right now that were scavenged from second-hand stores. The bald eagle is a powerful American totem. It represents strength and freedom. Because I see neither in America today, the eagle is both a sad symbol of what has been lost, and a beacon of what men must recover.

In October 2012, I gave two speeches. My scripts for both are found here. (The audiobook includes the "live" versions.)

The first speech was titled, "A Sky Without Eagles," and it sums up my disillusionment with The American Dream — the dissonance between what I value and what I see around and above me in the present.

"A Sky Without Eagles" was given to a private group of White Nationalists, and there are a few lines addressing the audience, but it is really about my failing faith in America as a nation. I think men of any ethnicity or race should be able to appreciate the emptiness in American "leadership" and "values." And, because globalism has created a similar absence of greatness in the leadership of many nations, there are many skies without eagles.

The second speech, titled, "The New Barbarians," looks to the future and a way out of Americanism — a way toward strength and freedom. Transcripts (or live recordings, in the audiobook) of both speeches are included here and they more or less bookend this collection.

Three completely new essays are included in this book.

The first is about weight training. People jump on all kinds of fitness bandwagons, but after working out for several years, I realized I was going to have to work out for the rest of my life. I started thinking about motivations for training. If you train, you should know why you train. I determined that I "Train for Honor."

I also thought it would be fun to explain my fixation on "CROM!" — Conan the Barbarian's god — after getting his name tattooed across my knuckles. This essay pretty well sums up my "spiritual" perspective.

Finally, I get a lot of questions from readers of *The Way of Men*, but a common one was "What kind of society would you really want?"

I've called myself an "Anarcho-Fascist," but only because I think the fasces symbolizes the essence of the primal male gang, and revitalizing tribal manliness will require a chaotic break from modernity. I'm not an anarchist or a fascist proper. I believe there's a "sweet spot" between complete chaos and over-civilized and mechanized bureaucracy. Thorstein Veblen called it "high barbarian" culture.

I put some thought into envisioning that "sweet spot" and decided to sketch out some of the features of the kind of tribe I'd want to belong to — the kind of tribe I think is "better" or "best." I decided to call it "The Brotherhood."

I don't recommend reading this collection straight through, because many themes — and even a few phrases — are repeated throughout. Flip through it and read the essays you haven't read, or the new ones, of your favorites, or the ones you forgot about. Then, some other day, read the first title that grabs you. Several essays do refer to ideas introduced in *The Way of Men*, and I would recommend reading that book before reading this one.

If you enjoy this book, please consider reviewing it or any book you enjoy online. It's the easiest and cheapest way to support independent authors and ideas that interfere with the mainstream media's regularly scheduled programming.

START THE WORLD!

Jack Donovan
Milwaukie, Oregon
Cascadia Bioregion
May 6, 2014.

VIOLENCE IS GOLDEN

A lot of people like to think they are "non-violent." Generally, people claim to "abjure" the use of violence, and violence is viewed negatively by most folks. Many fail to differentiate between just and unjust violence. Some especially vain, self-righteous types like to think they have risen above the nasty, violent cultures of their ancestors. They say that "violence isn't the answer." They say that "violence doesn't solve anything."

They're wrong. Every one of them relies on violence, every single day.

On election day, people from all walks of life line up to cast their ballots, and by doing so, they hope to influence who gets to wield the axe of authority. Those who want to end violence — as if that were possible or even desirable — often seek to disarm their fellow citizens. This does not actually end violence. It merely gives the state mob a monopoly on violence. This makes you "safer," so long as you don't piss off the boss.

All governments — left, right or other — are by their very nature coercive. They have to be.

Order demands violence.

A rule not ultimately backed by the threat of violence is merely a suggestion. States rely on laws enforced by men ready to do violence against lawbreakers. Every tax, every code and every licensing requirement demands an escalating progression of penalties that, in the end, must result in the forcible seizure of property or imprisonment by armed men prepared to do violence in the event of resistance or non–compliance. Every time a soccer mom stands up and demands harsher penalties for drunk driving, or selling cigarettes to minors, or owning a pit bull, or not recycling, she is petitioning the state to use force to impose her will. She is no longer asking nicely. The viability of every family law, gun law, zoning law, traffic law, immigration law, import law, export law and financial regulation depends on both the willingness and wherewithal of the group to exact order by force.

When an environmentalist demands that we "save the whales," he or she is in effect making the argument that saving the whales is so important that it is worth doing harm to humans who harm whales. The peaceful environmentalist is petitioning the leviathan to authorize the use of violence in the interest of protecting leviathans. If state leaders were to agree and express that it was, indeed, important to "save the whales," but then decline to penalize those who bring harm to whales, or decline to enforce those penalties under threat of violent police or military action, the expressed sentiment would be a meaningless gesture. Those who wanted to bring harm to whales would feel free to do so, as it is said, with impunity — without punishment.

Without action, words are just words. Without violence, laws are just words.

Violence isn't the only answer, but it is the final answer.

One can make moral arguments and ethical arguments and appeals to reason, emotion, aesthetics, and compassion. People are certainly moved by these arguments, and when sufficiently persuaded — providing of course that they are not excessively inconvenienced — people often choose to moderate or change their behaviors.

However, the willful submission of many inevitably creates a vulnerability waiting to be exploited by any one person who shrugs off social and ethical norms. If every man lays down his arms and refuses to pick them up, the first man to pick them up can do whatever he wants. Peace can only be maintained without violence so long as everyone sticks to the bargain, and to maintain peace every single person in every successive generation — even after war is long forgotten — must continue to agree to remain peaceful. *Forever and ever.* No delinquent or upstart may ever ask, "Or Else What?," because in a truly non-violent society, the best available answer is "Or else we won't think you're a very nice person and we're not going to share with you." Our troublemaker is free to reply, "I don't care. I'll take what I want."

Violence is the final answer to the question, "*Or else what?*"

Violence is the gold standard, the reserve that guarantees order. In actuality, it is better than a gold standard, because violence has universal value. Violence transcends the quirks of philosophy, religion, technology and culture. People say that music is a universal language, but a punch in the face hurts the same no matter what language you speak or what kind of music you prefer. If you are trapped in a room with me and I grab a pipe and gesture to strike you with it, no matter who you are, your monkey brain will immediately understand "or else what." And thereby, a certain order is achieved.

The practical understanding of violence is as basic to human life and human order as is the idea that fire is hot. You can use it, but you must respect it. You can act against it, and you can sometimes control it, but you can't just wish it away. Like wildfire, sometimes it is overwhelming and you won't know it is coming until it is too late. Sometimes it is bigger than you. Ask the Cherokee, the Inca, the Romanovs, the Jews, the Confederates, the barbarians and the Romans.

They all know *"Or else what."*
The basic acknowledgement that order demands violence is not a revelation, but to some it may seem like one. The very notion may make some people apoplectic, and some will furiously attempt to dispute it with all sorts of convoluted and hypothetical arguments, because it doesn't sound very "nice." But something doesn't need to be "nice" in order for it to be true. Reality doesn't bend over to accommodate fantasy or sentimentality.

Our complex society relies on proxy violence to the extent

that many average people in the private sector can wander through life without really having to understand or think deeply about violence, because we are removed from it. We can afford to perceive it as a distant, abstract problem to be solved through high-minded strategy and social programming. When violence comes knocking, we simply make a call, and the police come to "stop" the violence. Few civilians really take the time to think that what we are essentially doing is paying an armed band protection money to come and do orderly violence on our behalf. When those who would do violence to us are taken peacefully, most of us don't really make the connection, we don't even acknowledge to ourselves that the reason a perpetrator allows himself to be arrested is because of the gun at the officer's hip or the implicit understanding that he will eventually be hunted down by more officers who have the authority to kill him if he is deemed a threat. That is, if he is deemed a threat to order.

There are something like two and a half million people incarcerated in the United States. Over ninety percent of them are men. Most of them did not turn themselves in. Most of them don't try to escape at night because there is someone in a guard tower ready to shoot them. Many are "non-violent" offenders.

Soccer moms, accountants, celebrity activists and free range vegans all send in their tax dollars, and by proxy spend billions and billions to feed an armed government that maintains order through violence.

It is when our ordered violence gives way to disordered violence, as in the aftermath of a natural disaster, that we are forced to see how much we rely on those who maintain order through violence. People loot because they can, and kill because they think they'll get away with it. Dealing with violence and finding violent men who will protect you from other violent men suddenly becomes a real and pressing concern.

A pal once told me a story about an incident recounted by a family friend who was a cop, and I think it gets the point across.

A few teenagers were at the mall hanging out, outside a bookstore. They were goofing around and talking with some cops. The cop was a relatively big guy, not someone who you would want to mess around with. One of the kids told the cop that he didn't see why society needed police.

The cop leaned over and said to the spindly kid, "do you have any doubt in your mind about whether or not I could break your arms and take that book away from you if I felt like it?"

The teenager, obviously shaken by the brutality of the statement, said, "No."

"That's why you need cops, kid."

George Orwell wrote in his "Notes on Nationalism" that, for the pacifist, the truth that, "Those who 'abjure' violence can only do so because others are committing violence on their behalf," is obvious but impossible to accept. Much unreason flows from the inability to accept our passive reliance on violence for protection. Escapist fantasies of the John Lennon "Imagine" variety corrupt our ability to see the world as it is, and be honest with ourselves about the naturalness of violence to the human animal. There is no evidence to support the idea that man is an inherently peaceful creature. There is substantial evidence to support the notion that violence has always been a part of human life. Every year, archeologists unearth more primitive skulls with damage from weapons or blunt force trauma. The very first legal codes were shockingly grisly. If we feel less threatened today, if we feel as though we live in a non–violent society, it is only because we have ceded so much power over our daily lives to the state. Some call this reason, but we might just as well call it laziness. A dangerous laziness, it would seem, given how little most people say they trust politicians.

Violence doesn't come from movies or video games or music. Violence comes from people. It's about time people woke up from their 1960s haze and started being honest about violence again. People are violent, and that's OK. You can't legislate it away or talk your way around it. Based on the available evidence, there's no reason to believe that world peace will ever be achieved, or that violence can ever be "stopped."

It's time to quit worrying and learn to love the battle axe.

History teaches us that if we don't, someone else will.

A SKY WITHOUT EAGLES

This speech was given in early October, 2013, to a secret gathering of White Nationalists at an undisclosed location somewhere in the United States of America.

When modern, civilized, "progressive" people look to the Right, they see cruelty and hatred.

They call us "Little Hitlers."

"Little *Führers.*"

They believe that we're wannabe tyrants, dictators, bullies who want to "push people around" and "take their stuff." Everywhere we are portrayed as empty, sadistic monsters who are motivated only by personal gain and who experience joy only in the suffering of others.

There are men like that. Broken men. But not many.

I believe that most men are romantics, and the Right evokes a kind of *manly romanticism* — a particularly male sense of the Right order of things.

I should clarify what I mean by "The Right." I don't mean the "Old Right" or the "New Right" or even the "Alternative Right." What I mean most of all is the "Vertical Right," which isn't quite Right, but men who think vertically are placed on the Right, or accused of being on the Right, so it's the political shorthand everyone understands.

I got the idea of the "Alternative Vertical" from Colin Liddell's essay on *Alternative Right*.

He wrote:

> "If the Right Wing has an essence that most can agree on, it is hierarchy, natural inequality, meritocracy, and aspiration to the sacred, in other words a sense of the vertical.[1]"

So, by that definition, being on the Right isn't so much about being on my Right, or your Right. It's about a vision of human society that looks upward.

THE VERTICALLY ORIENTED MAN expects to look up and see his idea of greatness circling above him.

Because he knows in his heart that all men are NOT, in fact, created equal, the vertically oriented man understands that beneath the great, there will be men who are good, and average, and mediocre. There will also be the adequate, and the inadequate, and the sad, sorry failures. There will always be men who just didn't turn out, or even start out, very well.

1   Liddell, Colin. *Alternative Right*. March 4, 2013. "Alternative Vertical." http://www.radixjournal.com/altright-archive/altright-archive/main/the-magazine/alternative-vertical

The vertically oriented man can see a difference between fairness and absolute equality. He knows that justice isn't the same as sameness. The vertically oriented man wants all men to strive upward, to better themselves. But, he knows that to strive upward, you have to know which way is up, and which way is down.

THE HORIZONTALLY ORIENTED PERSON, however, is more concerned with the happiness of everyone within the group.

Because they are the most "at-risk," the horizontally oriented person is especially concerned with the feelings of weak, cowardly, inept and failed men (and women). He (or she) empathizes with them. Maybe he (or she) is one, and maybe he (or she) isn't, but his (or her) empathy for them causes him (or her) to see injustice in the just order of life.

The horizontally oriented person sees the sickly rabbit suffer, and to save that rabbit, he (or she) would shoot every single eagle out of the sky.

Instead of encouraging greatness, the horizontal thinker wants to redefine it, or handicap the great. He (or she) wants to "level the playing field" so that average men (and women) can play at being great and below average men (and women) can be saved from the emotional pain of knowing that they will never be great or even good.

In the horizontally oriented world, failures must be rewarded and re-imagined as successes. The victim is lauded for being a victim. The disabled are differently-abled. Being fat is fantastic. Every addiction, allergy, disease and delusion makes you special.

The problem with this arrangement in the natural world is that, as any vertically oriented man will tell you, when you take out the top of the food chain, your land will soon be overrun with rabbits, rats and other varmints. When you kill the eagles to save the hares, you end up knee-deep in rabbit shit.

That's what you get when the meek inherit the Earth — when things are out of balance.

In a balanced society, and in every balanced man, there is room for both vertical and horizontal thinking.

Horizontal thinking is essentially feminine, and is more concerned with nurturing and caring for all members of the tribe, from the newborn baby to the retired warrior who can no longer hunt or fight. The horizontal thinker is tuned in to the internal emotional life of the tribe, and only concerns herself (or himself) with danger when it is imminent and threatens everyone.

The horizontal thinker lives within the security zone created by the vertical thinker. Horizontal thinking is the product of peace and plenty. Horizontal thinking is a dependant's mind-set. Imagine a pregnant woman before modern medicine. A woman who is nursing or occupied with caring for young children. Her concerns are for the children, and she must trust that if there is an emergency or some kind of external threat, someone else will handle it. The horizontal thinker goes about her (or his) business, and trusts. Horizontal thinking is naturally optimistic. It assumes that everything will be okay, and concerns itself with promoting cheerfulness and good faith within the group.

Men, however, are natural pessimists. We know what evil lurks in our own hearts and we suspect the same of others. It has always been the job of men to prepare for and neutralize external threats. It has always been the first job of men to define the boundaries of the group — of "us" — and protect "us" from "them."

It is in the nature of man to look everywhere for threats, and it is an unfortunate side effect of his nature that he sometimes sees threats that aren't there. The vertical thinker has a hammer, and to him everything looks like a nail.

"I'm not sure what that is, but let's kill it just to make sure it doesn't come back and bite us on the ass later."

Man favors pre-emptive strike over "giving peace a chance," Because THEY ARE OUT THERE and YOU NEVER KNOW WHEN SOMETHING BAD IS GOING TO HAPPEN, the motto of the vertical thinker, like the Boy Scouts, is BE PREPARED.

Groups of men PREPARE by training, by pushing each other, by making sure every man is always at his best, and by making sure they know who the best men are — THEY WANT TO KNOW WHO THEY CAN DEPEND ON. Feelings are a luxury. Men cannot afford to be careless. They constantly test each other for loyalty, for competence, for fearfulness, for toughness.

These are the four TACTICAL VIRTUES I wrote about in *The Way of Men*.

STRENGTH. COURAGE. MASTERY. HONOR.

These virtues are first in the hierarchy of male virtues because they are survival virtues.

To the vertical thinker, hierarchy is OK.

"May the best man win."

No one likes losing — or not winning — but hierarchy is OK because ideally — and this a fairly romantic idea men have — every man SHOULD be trying his best whether he is winning or not.
Winning is relative. The collective goal is to be the best group. The collective result is what matters, and for our primal ancestors, the desired result was collective survival.

If you aren't the best, you don't wallow in it. You don't go crying to mom about it. You don't give up and let someone else handle it. You get over yourself and keep working to improve or do the best you can.

Life isn't fair, and maybe you aren't going to be the big dog, but it seems like the men in charge are the men who are the best at doing the things that matter most. Life isn't fair, but your brothers are counting on you, and you care what they think about you. You don't have to see yourself as a leader — a *Führer* — to see the value of natural hierarchy.

You don't have to be the biggest or the baddest to want to belong to a group that values STRENGTH, COURAGE, MASTERY and HONOR.

Wanting to belong to and be valued by a group that values and is known for STRENGTH, COURAGE, MASTERY and HONOR is a BASIC SURVIVAL INSTINCT for men.

Why would men want to belong to a group that is known for being weak, cowardly, inept and which suffers from an obvious lack of cohesion, shared values and internal loyalty? Belonging to a group like that would be a source of SHAME and DISHONOR. It's like being a member of a team that sucks.

If you're not in charge and you can't change the culture of the team, why wouldn't you start looking around for a gang or a team or a country or an ideology that DOES value the same things you do?

It is completely natural for people to wonder about your motivations. It's natural for them to assume that you are acting out of pure self interest. That's fair.

However, their characterizations of men on the Right may explain as much about their own vulgar, vengeful little hearts as about the motivations of vertical thinkers.

To be sure, men act — or try to act — to further their own interests. But not every "interest" is as base or direct as "push people around" or "get more stuff."
If that were so, heroism and self-sacrifice would be unheard of.

Men will die to save others. They'll die for honor. They'll die to avoid shame. They'll die for narrative. Men will risk death for a good story.

So, when men act in their own self-interest, their interests may be rather...abstract.

Masculine psychology isn't always as simple as "get more stuff" and "push people around." Self-interest could mean wanting to be part of a better team, a better society — a culture that values the same things you do in yourself and other men. Even if you don't get to "push people around" or "get more stuff."

I didn't move from the Left to the Right because I wanted to boss people around, or bully people. People on the Left do that plenty. Everybody likes winning, but I don't get my jollies watching people lose. I don't get any particular satisfaction out of watching people suffer. Unless they really, really deserve it.

NO, like many others, I'm drawn to the Right — to other vertical thinkers — because I want to look up and see greatness.

I'm not on the Right because I come from money or aristocracy. That's the OLD Right. I have no "entitlement" or "privilege" to protect. The men in my family have worked with their hands and their backs for hundreds of years. We've always been ruled by someone.

The majority of men have never been kings or tribal chieftains, and though we all have our moments, when I talk to other men on the Right — other vertical thinkers — I don't get a sense that any of us seriously wants to be a king or a dictator.

I don't want or need any power for myself that extends beyond a few hundred yards.

But, because maintaining any kind of order within human organizations requires violence — or the threat of violence — someone will always be required to wield the power of violence. Someone will have to hold the axe that answers the question "OR ELSE WHAT?"

If I have to bend my knee to someone, I want it to be someone worthy of my allegiance. If I must be ruled, I want to be ruled by men who are better men than I am. I want my rulers to represent the manly virtues of STRENGTH, COURAGE, MASTERY and HONOR, balanced with wisdom gained through experience. I want them to understand the world not just in theory, but in practice.

If I have to bend my knee, I want to look up and see eagles.

I want to live in a community that exalts strength, courage, mastery and honor in culture and art and architecture and education and law. That's my idea of a good tribe — a great society — a right and beautiful order of things.

I'm a romantic like that.

As I mentioned earlier, in a balanced, successful society – and in every balanced man – there is room for horizontal thinking. When threats are minimal and resources are plentiful, you can afford to worry about "feeling good." You can focus on the emotional life of the people inside the perimeter. You can afford to devote time and resources to other virtues. You can worry about being a "good" man.

If the men who wield the axe of power are LOYAL to their tribe —if they are men of HONOR, if they are VIGILANT and PROTECTIVE and COURAGEOUS and COMPETENT men, then there is room for horizontal thinking and making sure everyone is enjoying the group's prosperity.

Unfortunately, the modern world has been ruined by too much prosperity. Everything is too easy and men have allowed themselves to become dependants and to think like dependants.

Men became too optimistic and too trusting. Modern, civilized, "progressive" people have a near religious commitment to the idea that new ways are better than old ways, and that, no matter what happens, we are on some sort of pre-determined course to a future promised land that is, of course, better than where we are or where we have been. Because it's new. And that makes everyone "feel good."

Many call themselves "rational optimists," which never made much sense to me, because, you can't exactly call yourself rational if you've made a commitment to be optimistic whether it's rational or not. They are optimists because "feeling good" is what's important.

So people go to work and march forward with smiles on their faces and they cheer when someone crosses a marker on the road to PROGRESS.

A BLACK PRESIDENT.
A FEMALE PRESIDENT.
A TRANSGENDER PRESIDENT.
THE FIRST MENTALLY RETARDED PRESIDENT!

Why not? It's all about making people "feel good," right? It's all about breaking down boundaries and "re-thinking" values. You can't have winners and losers because losing makes people feel bad. SO EVERYONE WINS!

You can't have exclusive groups because excluding people makes people feel bad. You can't even have national borders because excluding people makes people feel bad. You have to include everyone in everything so no one feels bad.

It's mean if you only care about some people — if you only care about *your* people. So you have to care about everyone on the whole planet equally. All 7 OR SO BILLION OF

THEM...and counting.

The problem with that is that we are still very much a tribal species. According to Dunbar's number, our primal brains are only wired to care, really care, about 150 or so people.

Everything else is pretty much bullshit.

In an all-inclusive society that is all about feeling good, you end up with a lot of bullshitters. Everyone is bullshitting everyone and it's hard to tell if anybody really cares about anyone.

Since everyone is supposed to pretend to love everyone — *and no one really does* — we end up with a society that rewards people who pretend to care about everyone, but who really only care about money and status. We still have a hierarchy. It's just not based on strength or courage or honor.

When I look upward today, I see billionaires who are accountable to no group of people, who see themselves as "citizens of the world."

Instead of working for their neighbors, they can chuck some pocket change at some kids in Africa or build a new factory and give jobs to the working poor in some Third World country — where it also happens to be far more profitable.

And even that "fat cat," "robber baron" understanding of things is a bit quaint and 19th Century. It's not like we can fix this thing by storming a mansion and hanging a Carnegie or a Rockefeller or a Bloomberg.

The people who really run Western Civilization AREN'T EVEN PEOPLE. They are amoral transnational legal entities whose sole purpose is to grow and produce profit.

The people on the covers of our magazines, the people Americans are supposed to look up to — are CEOs and CFOs. They aren't the best men or the best women. They're just the best at making MONEY for big corporations — no matter how.

As Brad Pitt's character in *Killing Them Softly* said, "America's not a country. It's a business."

Because America's highest value is "feeling good," they'll do whatever is profitable and explain it away by telling us something that makes everyone feel good.

"Put a pink ribbon on it. Tell 'em we're fighting breast cancer. They LOVE that shit."

Who else am I supposed to bend my knee to in America?

Not the strongest men, the most honorable men, the most courageous men.
NO. Venal politicians and bureaucrats. Tools of corporations. Sociopaths who are dead inside and believe in nothing, who have only convictions of convenience, who change their minds whenever the wind blows or when someone yanks a chain..

Who else are we supposed to admire? Actors. Pretty, professional deceivers. The kind of people our ancestors treated with suspicion — like gypsies and whores. We're supposed to idolize men who play warriors in movies, while they send real warriors to die namelessly in some desert to protect the interests of big business.

And a little closer to the ground, who are you supposed to bend a knee to? Not the best men or the most courageous men or the most honorable men. Not people who really care about their people. No, mercenaries. Whoever takes that crappy job. The shoe-shine boys for the police state. Ticket writers and paper pushers and rule-citers. A DMV as far as the eye can see. You've been to the airport. Who gets to push you around?

This civilization became too successful, too dependent, too trusting, too optimistic. Too many of us became horizontal thinkers — too worried about making everyone "feel good." And the wealthy — the corporations — want us to keep "feeling good."

They want us to stay dependent and weak. They fund a toady class of academics to flatter them with feel-good TED talks and teach the evils of nationalism, tribalism, violence, and masculine virtue. They hire and applaud professional feminists who go around to schools and teach boys that they have to "re-imagine" masculinity in a non-threatening way — a servile, dependent way that has nothing to do with STRENGTH, COURAGE, MASTERY or HONOR.

Of course they do.

Of course they want to neutralize the group of men who pose the biggest threat to their place in the financial hierarchy. Of course they want to emasculate groups of men who could threaten their interests.

When I look up in America — *America the business* —that's what I see. Those are the kind of people who hold the axe of power. When I look upward in America — I see a sky without eagles.

And that's why I support you fine folks here today. I'm not interested in hate or cruelty. I support all kinds of tribalism and nationalism. I support human-scale groups of people who actually care about each other. I support people who support hierarchical, patriarchal tribes of vertical thinkers who want to look up and see STRENGTH, COURAGE, MASTERY and HONOR.

Because I'm a romantic like that.

ANARCHO-FASCISM

"In a society that has abolished every kind of adventure the only adventure that remains is to abolish that society."

— Situationist graffiti, May 1968

As a political ideology, fascism was a mixed bag of 20th Century ideas. Its athletic presence hung with flirty, politically expedient schemes like universal suffrage, and in many ways last century's fascism was defined by its responses to other political movements of the time — like Marxism and liberal capitalism.

But, just beyond the historical details of fascism, there is something eternal. Italian writer Umberto Eco called it "*Ur-fascism*" — meaning "primitive" or "original." Unfortunately, his snatchy "fourteen points" were overly concerned with the top-down totalitarianism of fascism's notable dictators and their party boys. His "*ur-fascism*" wasn't "primitive" enough. It wasn't "eternal" at all.

The word "fascism" has become sloppy shorthand for any

violent, intrusive police state. For most, fascism evokes a people forced into lockstep conformity by an all-powerful government. 20th Century political fascism had many other features, and they were instituted differently in different nations. Oppressive, runaway governments are also not unique to 20th Century fascism. Marxism, Catholicism and Islam have all produced cruel, iron-fisted police states. If being more afraid of your own government than you are of its external enemies is a measure of totalitarian tyranny, America's own "progressive" surveillance state is headed that way. Fascism and totalitarianism may be confused in the popular imagination, but they aren't the same thing.

The fasces was a powerful symbol before Mussolini was born, so it is possible to separate the symbol from his regime and see it in its own right. I am not concerned so much with the usage of the fasces as a symbol of magisterial power in Republican Rome. I am more interested in the phenomenon this pre-Roman symbol appears to represent. Fascism has been described as a "male fantasy," and I agree that the fasces symbolizes a distinctly male worldview. What is it about the fasces that captures the male imagination?

Most people associate the "evils" of fascism with a top-down bureaucratic institution, but to me the fasces itself appears to symbolize a bottom-up idea.

The bound rods of the fasces represent strength and the authority of a unified male collective. That's its "primitive" appeal. True tribal unity can't be imposed from above. It's an organic phenomenon. Profound unity comes from men bound together by a red ribbon of blood. The blood of dire necessity that binds the band of brothers becomes the blood of heritage and duty that ties the family, the tribe, the nation. The fasces captures the male imagination because it appears to symbolize the unified will of men. Men prefer to believe that they offer their allegiance by choice, whether they truly do or not. Free association — or the appearance of it — is the difference between free men and slaves. If you can't just walk away, you're a prisoner. If you choose to stay, if you choose to align your fate to the fate of the group and submit to the collective authority of the group, you are a member, not a slave. As a member, you add the weight of your manhood to a unified confederacy of men.

The fasces became a popular decorative motif for American government buildings in the 19th and early 20th Centuries, and its symbolism is consistent with an earlier Latin motto adopted by the union: e pluribus unum. "Out of many, one." 20th Century political fascism itself was preceded by the Italian fascio—voluntary "bundles" or unions of men uniting to assert their collective interests. Mussolini was a member of a fascio before he was a "fascist." This idea of men choosing to band together and increase their strength was most eloquently explained by the ape "Caesar" in *Rise of the Planet of the Apes (2011)*. Breaking a single stick, and then gathering a bundle, Caesar shows his imprisoned comrades that, "Ape alone...weak...apes together...strong."

When the fasces is revered, it symbolizes "our power." When the fasces is reviled, it is despised because it has become a symbol of "their power."

Virile men do not unite to become sandbags. The fasces symbolizes men bound together with an axe, ready for action, issuing a threat of violence — of "or else." The fasces is a warning, a promise of retaliation, a paddle on the wall for traitors, slackers and law-breakers.

In *The Way of Men*, I wrote that "The Way of Men is The Way of the Gang." Primal masculinity is rooted in the practical, tactical ethos of a gang of men struggling to survive and triumph over external forces.

From this perspective, I see the fasces as a "universal gang sign." It symbolizes, better than any other symbol I can think of, the moment when men tie their fates together and align themselves against nature, against other men, against…the world. The fasces depicts the genesis of "us," of "our team," of "our culture," of "our honor" — the formation of a collective identity. It symbolizes then moment when the war of all against all becomes a war of men against men, of "us" against "them." The fasces symbolizes the moment when men create order from chaos.

This pure, primal manliness can only be realized under stress. It can only rise out of chaos, as a reaction to external forces. From there it matures, shaped by time, into an honor culture, and from that culture — that combination of collective history and custom that characterize the identity of a people — comes Tradition. Everything I recognize as good and worth saving about men and masculinity thrives in this cultural sweet spot between the purity of the warrior-gang and the spoiled, conniving depravity of complex merchant-based cultures.

With no more frontiers to explore, save space — which can only be allowed, even in fantasy, as a neutered bureaucratic project — the modern, effeminate, bourgeois "First World" states can no longer produce new honor cultures. New, pure warrior-gangs can only rise in anarchic opposition to the corrupt, feminist, anti-tribal, degraded institutions of the established order. Manhood can only be rebooted by the destruction of their future, and the creation of new futures for new or reborn tribes of men. It is too late for conservatism. For the majority of men, only occupied structures and empty gestures remain.

The way of men can only be rediscovered in Night and Chaos.

Ur-fascism is the source of honor culture and authentic patriarchal tradition.

Ur-fascism is a response to anarchy.

The political position of *The Way of Men* is "anarcho-fascist."

This *anarcho-fascism* is not an end; it is hungry for a new beginning.

START THE WORLD!

The secrets of the hoarie deep, a dark
Illimitable Ocean without bound,
Without dimension, where length, breadth, & highth,
And time and place are lost; where eldest Night
And Chaos, Ancestors of Nature, hold
Eternal Anarchie, amidst the noise
Of endless Warrs, and by confusion stand.

— Milton, *Paradise Lost*

MIGHTY WHITE

I started rubbing elbows with White Nationalists a few years ago.

I call 'em "The Mighty Whites."

I support White Nationalists. They are not all equally right about everything, but I am sympathetic to many of their general aims.

I think white people should be able to organize and advance their own interests just like every other group of people. For those of my readers who might be concerned, I want to explain why.

Ten out of ten minorities agree that being a minority can really blow. As an ambassador for a smaller group, you carry the baggage for all of "your kind." As a minority, you have to work twice as hard to disprove negative stereotypes. You spend a lot of time dispelling misconceptions or explaining things. It's annoying and tedious.

Stereotyping and prejudgment is a survival tactic. It's natural, it's human, and it's not going away. The people who say they are opposed to stereotyping do it just as much as everyone else. Have you ever listened to an "objective" atheist rant about evangelical Christians? A casual conversation with an enlightened Northerner about the South might lead you to believe that strange fruit still swings there from every poplar tree. After living in San Francisco for a few years I determined that most residents of fog city had scribbled "Thar be dragons!" over at least forty states.

Humans are tribal. We need an "us," and those who are not us must be "them." We form tribal bubbles, and we filter out information that doesn't confirm our biases about others. We associate with people who look like we do, or think like we do, or believe what we believe. Most of us do this even when we are trying consciously not to.

It's easy enough to maintain the illusion of "one world tribe" when you are sitting in a polite, politically correct office, sipping a latte with a cherry-picked collection of educated and carefully groomed people from other groups.

In the land of calloused hands and cheap coffee, folks stick to their own kind. As a blue collar guy I can relate well enough to other groups. My pap worked on the railroad his whole life, and like him, when I punch the clock I have to learn to get along with whomever the boss hires, or work just gets a lot harder.

I have a lot of experience working with Mexicans. They're funny, happy, hard working and easy to get along with. But I'm not a Mexican. I'm not one of them. We can have a laugh over something universal, but they have different lifeways and for the most part they stick together. Sure, I could learn Spanish. I make tasty carnitas and I like drinking margaritas in the sun. But, like the man said, sticking a feather up your butt does not make you a chicken. I'll always be a gringo.

I like being a gringo just fine. I feel more at home with white folks of my class and background than I do with people from other groups. Plenty of crackers are total assholes, but at least I know how to read them better. Kipling got exemplary man-hood right with "If," and he got in-group affinity right with "The Stranger."

> The Stranger within my gate,
> He may be true or kind,
> But he does not talk my talk—
> I cannot feel his mind.
> I see the face and the eyes and the mouth,
> But not the soul behind.
>
> The men of my own stock,
> They may do ill or well,
> But they tell the lies I am wonted to,
> They are used to the lies I tell;
> And we do not need interpreters
> When we go to buy or sell.

When times get tough or the shit hits the fan, I think human groups shake out pretty much the way they do in prison: race, religion, ideology, class. Helter skelter. When everyone has the same race and religion, we still find reasons to separate ourselves into smaller tribal groups. The English, the French, ze Germans. English colonists vs. English monarchists. Jocks vs. nerds.

If you want me to hand you a set of finger paints, tell me that race is "just about skin color." If you actually believe that in 2011, you belong at the kiddie table watching "Dora the Explorer." Race is hereditary. So are a lot of other human qualities. You get some of your parents' strengths and some of their weaknesses. Race is about your family, and your family's family, and your family's family's family. Your race is part of your heritage, passed down to you from those who came before. Race, culture, history and tradition combine to give you a sense of being part of an ethnic group.

From 100 yards away, the first things you'll notice about me are that I am white and I am male. That's where my taxonomy starts. If I were seen committing a crime, the cops would be looking for a white male, about 5'10-5'11, bald, 200 pounds, average build, with tattoos.

If I live to be 70, in my lifetime white men will be a minority in the United States. Whites are already a minority in many American cities. White men make up 30% of the population in Baltimore, 40% in Philadelphia, 39% in Atlanta. If you want to know what it feels like to be a minority, go to those places and look for a working class job.
Even in places where whites are still a majority, like San Di-

ego, whole segments of the workforce are dominated by certain groups. I looked for work in San Diego a few years ago.

On any given day, Portland tends to have as many or more jobs in the General Labor category of Craigslist than San Diego. The Portland metro area has about 2 million people. San Diego has about 3 million people. There are one million more people in San Diego, but the same amount of general labor jobs get posted. In part, this is because San Diego's population of legal and illegal Mexican immigrants creates a situation where Pedro always has a cousin who has another cousin who needs a job. Openings for a lot of jobs never go public. I see it happen all the time here in Portland, too.

There's nothing wrong with that. Why shouldn't Pedro try to get his cousin's cousin a job? Why shouldn't they help each other out? Why shouldn't they take care of their own? Only white people are stupid enough to feel guilty about doing that. Do you think a black man is going to feel bad about helping out a brotha, even in Baltimore — where blacks make up almost 70% of the population?

Every ethnic group in America is taught to be proud of their race and ethnicity, except white people. America has black television channels, black magazines, black community organizations, black lobbying groups, black scholarships and black barber shops. Any black who wants to can go to a major city and disappear into an almost completely black community. Same thing for the varied Hispanic groups. Asians are far more financially successful, but they too are often insular and protective of their race and heritage. All of these groups recognize that they share some common ancestry and some common interests, and they organize to assert those interests. If you take a political editorial or press release put out by an Hispanic, black, Asian or even a gay publication and replace the group name with "white," to the average American eye it will read like it was written by David Duke or George Lincoln Rockwell.

The flimsy rationales for why it is not acceptable for white groups to speak or organize in the same way are based on notions of white majority, white privilege and white cultural dominance. However, whites are no longer a majority in many places, and as any of the "99%" will tell you, average white people aren't running the show. The white country club set doesn't give a damn about what happens to most of us. A lot of them have realized that "diversity" policies work in their favor—especially when they want to export jobs, hire cheap labor or avoid expensive lawsuits. And, thanks to the "arc of history" civil rights narrative that the media loves to promote, rich white people can shit on poor white people and feel like they are doing God's work.

A multicultural, multiracial, melting pot society that forbids only one ethnic group from preserving its culture and organizing to further its own interests is criminally hypocritical. I have a low tolerance for swindling and deception, and the amount of double-talk and outright lying employed to maintain that hypocrisy is despicable.

So many white people have prejudices against other groups of people, choose to live in white neighborhoods, prefer their children to date other whites, and surround themselves with other white people. Some even (privately) make racist jokes.

When asked about race, these same self-righteous whites will dutifully denounce racism, white privilege, and white identity in all its forms — just like their expensive professors told them to. They come off like Patrick Bateman in *American Psycho*, who recites the social causes of the day to keep people from guessing he's a completely opportunistic sociopath who will tell people whatever he thinks they want to hear.

Any white person who talks about being white like it is anything other than a cross to bear, or even half-heartedly suggests the idea of organizing as a white group, or even points out a "hate fact" like the black-on-white crime rate will be publicly shamed, excluded and can easily be fired from his or her job.

Social courage isn't the highest form of courage, but it's something.

Being a white anti-racist is the easiest thing to be in the world. It's like being a papist in Vatican City. There's nothing brave about it. It's the *status quo*. You're just doing what you've been told to do, whether it makes sense or not.

Challenging the deeply entrenched anti-white bias of multiculturalist orthodoxies is heroic by comparison. I may not agree with everything that every white nationalist says—they have their own noble lies—but I applaud any white man or woman who is willing to stand up for their own people and challenge some of the greatest lies of our time.

I am not a white supremacist.

I don't feel the need to try to prove that my team is objective-ly better in every way than every other team. Sure, there are probably some bell-curve type differences between the major races. I am also sure I can find a person of just about any race who is better than me at just about anything. Whether white people are superior or not isn't the point.

The point is that white people are my people. We're an eth-nic and racial group with a common heritage. Because ste-reotypes aren't going away, because humans are tribal, and because we're a group that is well on its way to becoming just another minority, we have every right to organize as a group and take care of our own. I'm pro-white because I am pro-me. I'm pro-my family. I'm in favor of remembering my ancestors in a positive light. I support the preservation of my people's history and culture, and I resist the revisionism of groups who wish to skew history to favor the interests of others. I know that the accomplishments of great white men are not my personal achievements, and I know I can't trade on them as if they entitle me to special treatment, but these things are just as important to my identity as the histories of other people are to their identities.

I believe that people should form groups that suit them and exclude others if they believe it is in their benefit to do so. On that note, I can tell you that not all of the Mighty Whites want me around. Every so often, some hysterical prig sallies forth from his Arthurian fap den to proclaim me a he-man woman hater, a Satanist, a sodomite, and a threat to the cause. I'm flattered that they think I'm a big enough deal to sink their battleship, but if that's the case, they are already well and truly fucked. I am pro-white and I support WNs because I'm white and because I think they are right about a lot of things—not because I expect them all to send me love letters. That said, most of the WNs and pro-whites I've dealt with have been decent, straightforward, polite and helpful.

I am pro-white, but race is not my favorite issue to write about. Race is not what I spend the majority of my time thinking about. If anything, I know too well that it distracts people from the bulk of my work.

My work is about men. It's about understanding masculinity and the plight of men in the modern world. It's about what all men have in common. My research and thinking in this area have led me to the conclusion that men are tribal. Women are tribal, too, but women logically tend to favor material security over tribal loyalty. Most men feel more alive, more confident and more comfortable in their own skins when they have a sense of belonging within a group of men.

The concept of honor as I understand it cannot exist without some sense of tribal membership, whether based on race or religion or class or some other form of identification. In both old New York City and old Japan, groups of firemen used to fight each other.

Honor requires a group of men who will judge you, who will threaten you with exclusion and shame, but who will also push you beyond your comfort zone and reward your efforts with respect and loyalty. Manliness and honor are hierarchical. Honor is incompatible with enforced "equality" and it is incompatible with enforced inclusiveness.

I don't know if what I've written here qualifies me as a White Nationalist or not. I'm in no hurry to become a card-carrying member for any organization or movement. As a writer, I'm just trying to be honest, to say what I mean and mean what I say. That takes me to some unusual places and puts me in touch with unusual people.

I'm OK with that.

VOTE WITH YOUR ASS

"Hey man, I still think we can turn this thing around."

That's what your vote says.

That's what you're telling people when you argue in favor of a candidate, or against one. You're saying that a change in management could, at least potentially, create a better future. It's not the system that's broken; it's those head-niggas-in-charge who are ruinin' everything. The bright idea is that if we get their guy out and put our guy in—our nigga—he could really turn things around.

Where, exactly, is your nigga gonna turn it to?

How far is he going to turn back the clock? How much cleaning up are they going to let him do? How many agencies is he going to close? How many amendments is he going to repeal? How many policies is he going to change, and why is he going to do these things for you? What's in it for him?

Let's say there's an honest man in the race. Let's just say there is—for the sake of argument.

Let's say it for the laughs.

Let's just say there is an honest man in the race who believes in the things that you believe in, a guy who is on your side. Let's imagine a candidate—because there isn't one, not one—who is willing to take a stand against global business conglomerates that wield more power than most nations. Let's imagine a nationalist candidate—an anti-globalist who isn't going to make things easier for companies to export jobs, import cheap goods, and price Americans out of their own market. Let's imagine there's a guy who is actually willing to draw a line where our borders are supposed to be and say "no more."

Conjure in your mind, if you will, a fella who is going to side with men when women want something—who won't beta down and give in every time women nag him a little. I'm trying to keep this fantasy realistic, so let's not get crazy. Let's not get into divorce laws or domestic violence polices or sexual discrimination lawsuits or women in the military. Just try to imagine a guy who can stand up and say that men ought to feel free to exclude women from a private golf club if they want to. Imagine that guy—because he's about the best you can hope for.

This guy, your best hope, is going to get up every morning and tell companies wielding the wealth of nations and 51% of the voting population to go fuck themselves, because he's on *your side*.

You see how unrealistic that is, right?

Funny stuff.

What's your best-case-scenario for America? I think the best that most men can reasonably hope for is for this thing to keep limping along and not get too much worse—that we'll still be able to find a way to make it, to play the system and win sometimes.

(Some men will inevitably prosper no matter how bad things get for most men. Maybe you want to be that guy. Good on 'ya. The point here is about changes in your odds.)

The likelihood of feminist laws being rolled back, even as far as the 1980s, is slim. The best you can hope for from elected officials—who also depend on the votes of women—is to fend off deep, hen-pecked "Swedish" feminism.

Whites are going to become minorities in a lot of areas, and hopefully being a minority white man who isn't wealthy won't suck too much. We can hope that all of the "youths" and "vibrants" who have been taught that we are their natural oppressors—and that we are naturally to blame for everything bad that happens to them—will be kind and benevolent to us. We can hope that they won't hold a grudge or take advantage of us or attack us in an angry mob whenever the media winds them up.

We can hope that we'll still have the right to bear arms and defend ourselves, and that we'll be treated fairly by a legal system run by and for others. The average guy can hope that judges and legislators will at least be reminded of the Constitution when they give decisions and write laws.

We can hope that freedom of speech will outlast us. We know that writing or saying the wrong thing may get us fired, but we can hope that they won't put us in prison for it, like they do in more "evolved" nations like France, Germany, or England.

Basically, we can take a conservative position. We can try to hold on to what remains from the past and what is good in the present. We can vote to keep things from changing too much, too fast. Maybe, if we're really lucky, we'll be able to regain some ground every once in a while — to right some wrongs, to correct some errors. Voting for the guy who is going to fuck things up the least is a conservative position.

Progressives—feminists, multiculturalists, socialists, and others—are more enraptured by their leaders and more excited about the future because they have an end goal in mind. They aren't voting to keep things from getting too much worse, they are voting to achieve a State of Kumbaya. In the State of Kumbaya, every person of every sex and race is equal in every which way. Everyone shares and shares alike, and no one has a bad word to say about anyone else. In Kumbaya, there is no one to kill or die for (and no religion, too). This is not a radical position, because it is more or less the official position, but people who vote toward Kumbaya are still voting forward.

Conservatives vote to block them, or to go backward. They vote to restore, reclaim, and prevent. Conservatives believe that they can still turn this thing around.

I'm not a conservative.

I don't believe we can turn this thing around by voting to put a new head-nigga-in-charge.

I'm not going to argue with you about why this nigga is better than that nigga.

I'll be sitting it out entirely.

From now on, I'm voting with my ass.

I'm not advocating apathy. I don't want you to stop caring. I want you to stop believing.

Voting implies consent. It implies that you still believe in the system and that you are satisfied with your options.

I want you to withdraw your consent.

In 2008, voter turnout was around 57%. That's actually high for elections in recent years, and for a variety of reasons I doubt we'll see that kind of enthusiasm again soon. However, the fact that we are being governed with the active consent of less than 60% of the population is worth consideration. In 1924, less than 49% of the voting age population turned out to elect an established incumbent challenged by a lackluster candidate who was actually a compromise between two other deadlocked candidates. 2012 looks like a great year to aim for under 50% again.

Let the head-nigga-in-charge claim he has a mandate from the people, when half of the voting age population couldn't be bothered to vote either for or against him. And this isn't even about him. It's not about any one candidate. It's about a system that can only produce globalists to act in our national interests. It's about a system that makes it easier for men to pander to women than it is for them to stand up for men.

America is losing faith in its public institutions. In a 2011 Gallup poll, only 12% expressed "a great deal" or "quite a lot" of confidence in Congress. 35% had faith in the presidency, 37% in the Supreme Court. As few had confidence in newspapers (28%) as they did in television news (27%). Less than 30% trusted the criminal justice system, the banks, the unions or big business.

Withdrawing your support for America's political system is a more powerful statement than your vote.

Not voting is a vote of "no confidence."

Your vote isn't going to turn this thing around. The best thing you can do for your country — for the men around you, for the future — is to let the system tear itself apart. The way to increase personal sovereignty for men is to decrease the sovereignty of the state by withdrawing the consent of the governed. Sure, this could and probably will result in naked power grabs by "elected" officials. These actions will only decrease confidence further. That's short-term. I'm thinking about the long game. If American men stop thinking of the government as "us" and start thinking of it as "them" — if we stop thinking of ourselves as Americans and start acting in our own interests, things could get really interesting.

So this year, don't argue about politics.

Don't vote.

Vote with your ass.

Or, if you really want to vote, don't vote for any of the official candidates. Have fun with it. Vote for a write-in.

Vote for Zod. Vote for Cthulu. Vote for Crom. Vote for fucking Cobra Commander for all I care.

Just don't vote for any of the assholes on the ballot.

THE GRIEVANCE TABLE
Why I Am Not A "Men's Rights Activist"

During my research for what became *The Way of Men*, I became increasingly aware of anti-male bias in American culture, education, academia and law. What moved me the most were stories of fathers having their kids taken away by lying, vengeful ex-wives, or being financially crippled by impossible-to-pay child support payments arranged by a family court system that favors women. Fatherless families create so many problems, especially for fatherless sons, and many of these guys who actually *want* to be good fathers to their children are being prevented from spending time with their kids.

I started talking to Bill Price, who at the time had just started running a blog about men's issues called *The Spearhead*. During the break-up of his first marriage, Bill was arrested at gunpoint after his wife made what she later admitted (without penalty) were bogus claims about him to the police. Men face a lot of problems today, but the prospect of being arrested at the mere word of a woman is an evil injustice.

In October 2009, I started writing for *The Spearhead*. Many *Spearhead* readers consider themselves "Men's Rights Activists," or "MRAs." MRAs point out the duplicity of feminists, expose unfairness in the legal system and draw attention to misandry (the hatred or dislike of boys or men) in the mainstream media. Like White Nationalists, they send out an interference signal that undermines the "noble lies" of American progressivism.

I agree that men and manliness are often mocked by smug misandrists and sex traitors in the media. I sympathize with fathers and divorced men who have been screwed over by family courts and our current legal system, which favors women. Women have established massive organizations, many of which are wholly or partially taxpayer funded — to serve their own interests at the expense of the interests of men. Many balk at the idea that men even have any legitimate interests of their own. But men are not women, and they do have different interests. Because their interests are not being addressed, Western men are collectively faltering.

The powers that be have finally learned to leverage the noblest instincts of men against them. Men are told to deal with it, to handle it. No whining. Just take it, to prove that you can. To prove that you're better, that you're stronger. Shoulder it.

I agree with MRA's about many things and see many of the same problems, but I cannot call myself a "Men's Rights Activist."

The sticking point for me is the whole "rights" thing.

The notion of "unalienable rights" is an Enlightenment-era

rhetorical flourish that has been abused to the point of absurdity. The idea that men or women have "natural rights" is a myth, handily debunked by L.A. Rollins, among others.

"The metaphorical nature of natural rights is obvious in many statements by natural rights mythologizers. Consider a few examples. According to Ronald Dworkin, Individual rights are political trumps held by individuals. But will Dworkin's individual rights literally trump the guns held by a bunch of cops enforcing an 'unjust' law? Can shrimps whistle? John Hospers writes, "And so I put up a 'no trespassing' sign, which marks off the area of my right. Each individual's right is his 'no trespassing' sign in relation to me and others." Of course, unlike a real, literal 'no trespassing' sign, natural rights are invisible. But what use is an invisible 'no trespassing' sign? Another natural rights mythologizer is Eric Mack who says, "Lockean rights alone provide the moral and philosophical barrier against the state's encroachment upon society." But a 'moral philosophical barrier' is merely a metaphorical barrier, and it will no more prevent the state's encroachment upon 'Society' than a moral philosophical shield will stop an arrow from piercing your body."

— L.A. Rollins
The Myth of Natural Rights and Other Essays

Men have no natural rights. They have no natural right to father their children, or to be heads of their households. They have no natural right to marry, or to have sex, or to "pursue happiness." Men are animals vying with each other for resources, like every other animal. The United Nations invented a bunch of magic human rights that people "should" have, and it's telling that most of the states in the world disagree on one point or another. Some of the supposed "human rights" don't even make a whole lot of sense, and most are merely pleasant ideas. A state serves its own interests, and the foremost interest of any state is to remain in power.

Government is by its very nature coercive. Freedom is a relative term. Freedom within a state means that you are able to do certain things, but you give up the "right" to do other things. A state cannot offer true "freedom." At least not to everyone. A state offers order in exchange for obedience. *Ordered violence.* You pay the state with your taxes. For your money and your obedience, the state promises to hurt people before — or after — they hurt you. The state will not always make good on this promise. But it's the best racket in town. And anyway, like any working mob, your allegiance is considered mandatory — the state is also selling protection from itself.

So you pay up, and you do fine so long as you don't give no lip to the wrong guys.

They'd be the guys with guns. The guys licensed to hurt people for you.

(Or the guys who are in with the guys with guns.)

When you pay your taxes, you tacitly fund the deeds of men (and women) who are willing to dispense violence on your behalf — so as you don't have to get your pretty little hands dirty. You also get to keep your stuff. And if you are wronged, you go to the racket to ask for "justice."

Men used to run the state, so they enjoyed a favored position in many respects. It asked the most from them, but also flattered their egos and gave them a certain amount of autonomy at home.

When men offered to split the run of the state with women, they divided the state's interests.

Men tend to want more independence and autonomy. Manliness requires action and risk — risk with the potential of failure. Men of worth crave the opportunity to succeed or fail on their own merits. As the social democratic state expands, it offers more services, more safety nets, more regulations, and fewer opportunities for risk. The good guys who came by once a month to offer you a little protection and sanity are now hovering over your shoulder all day long and offering to wipe and powder your ass. Men are generally the ones you'll find grumbling about these little indignities as they accumulate. They feel stunted, hemmed in, powerless. This puts them at odds with the state.

Women on the other hand, as all of human history has shown, are more or less happy to be dependent, so long as they enjoy a certain level of comfort and security. They have a greater aversion to risk–they want to protect people from the consequences of their own bad decisions. They're more empathic — they want to see everyone cared for. They're less thumotic

— they're frightened by the displays of volatile, spirited anger that men applaud. Women are good at working within a system. This is why women love socialism. They're abandoning men for the state, because the state is big and powerful and smooth-talking and rich and it says it wants to take care of them forever and ever.

As has often been said, "Security+power+money = gina tingles."

Women's desire to be cared for and their support for the state's growth ultimately gives them a position of favor within the new state.

In the case of "men's rights," this is where I see some inherent difficulty.

And I have to ask, men:

Is this really what you want–another place at "The Grievance Table,"another empty bowl, another list of complaints?

An appointment to whisper in the headmistress's ear, seeking favors or redress?

Men made this world in their own image. Men invented the game and ran the racket. Until a generation or two ago, they sat at the heads of their own tables. They're the stronger 49% of the population, not a tiny, oppressed minority. If the state no longer serves the interests of men, if they must grovel and petition for "rights", maybe men should start thinking "regime change," or better, "paradigm shift."

The civil rights paradigm is built around the assumption that men, especially heterosexual white men, are the universal oppressors, the source of all true evil. It's a movement to remove you from power. It's not designed to address your grievances. It won't restore what it sees as lost "privilege." And in determining what is fair and what is "privilege," the reigning civil rights paradigm is necessarily biased. The only help it dares provide is to assist you in accepting your reduced status — through re-education or therapy. Those who say that you must lower your expectations and abandon your ideals are not friends, but castrating agents of your serpentine masters. These solutions are merely anesthetic.

It is neither acceptable, nor in the best nature of men that they should resign themselves to being mere supplicants in every aspect of life.

I suggest that the civil "rights" seeking posture cannot succeed for men–especially when they seek the favor and permission of women–and that it would be better to consider a bolder, more authoritative stance.

"...since Fortune changes and men stand fixed in their old ways, they are prosperous so long as there is congruity between them, and the reverse when there is not. Of this, however, I am well persuaded, that it is better to be impetuous than cautious. For Fortune is a woman who to be kept under must be beaten and roughly handled; and we see that she suffers herself to be more readily mastered by those who so treat her than by those who are more timid in their approaches. And always, like a woman, she favors the young, because they are less scrupulous and fiercer, and command her with greater audacity."

— Niccolo Machiavelli, *The Prince*

THERE IS NO HONOR
IN COMPETITION WITH
WOMEN

I understand honor as a system of accounting for men's souls. There are credits and debits, investments, loans, outstanding debts. Honor is gained, wagered, lost and regained. In the best case scenario, a man accumulates enough wealth to withstand inevitable short-term losses and indignities. Substantial achievements offer a cushion, a safety net pop psychologists refer to as "security." Luxury is not having to worry about the little stuff.

Like my pal's dad. He volunteered for a second tour in 'Nam so his brother wouldn't have to go. So what if he reps out his bench presses with ABBA blaring in his headphones. He earned it, and he sure as hell doesn't need my approval. Not too many guys have portfolios that contain *valor* these days.

Honor can be a confusing term because it is often used so casually. At the most mundane level it has come to mean merely "good" or "to hold in high esteem." Honor roll, "honor diversity," "honor the earth," "Honor Golden Retrievers." I am speaking of honor in a less pedestrian sense.

James Bowman, in his *Honor – A History*, wrote about both *reflexive* honor and *cultural honor*. Bowman's reflexive honor could also be described as "face"— the need to respond to an attack or an insult to avoid looking weak or inferior. His cultural honor "comprises the traditions, stories and habits of a particular society about (among other things) the proper and improper uses of violence." He also reminds readers in his introduction to the concept that "in spite of the discrediting that honor has undergone, the basic honor of the savage — bravery for men, chastity for women — is still recognizable beneath the surfaces of the popular culture that has done so much to efface it. If you doubt it, try calling a man a wimp or a woman a slut."

Building on Bowman's ideas, a man's honor is his private and public sense of worth as a man. Honor is a reputation for strength and the courage to use it when necessary to defend that sense of masculinity.

When men compete with each other, provided that it is a fair fight — "apples to apples" — men gain honor for more than just winning. They gain honor from having the courage to fight in the first place, for what dog fighters call "gameness" — perseverance, spunk, determination. Men respect other men who show courage, even if they almost always lose. Men in competition with each other are esteemed, win or lose, for good sportsmanship, fairness, heart, even compassion — all aspects of Bowman's cultural honor.

One time I ended up in a half-drunken sparring match with a buddy of mine. He loved to fence with shinai, and no one else at the party would do it. So I went out and played samurai with him for a few minutes. His bamboo sword left my forehead bleeding. But that didn't matter. I knew I gained his respect and we became better friends that night. Poetically, our friendship also ended over a matter of honor, years later.

Competition with women is almost always a net loss of honor for a man. Men don't consider competition between men and women to be "apples to apples." I don't think women do either.

To clarify, I'm not talking about "play" competition. Playing against your girl on a video game or a board game or miniature golf doesn't count. I'm talking about competition that matters.

A woman has much to gain and very little to lose by competing with a man who she thinks she can beat. No one will think her less of a woman for losing, because womanhood has nothing to do with competing with men. But if she beats a man, it will be a triumph of David over Goliath. Men will cheer her on, because in squaring off with a man she shows courage, and everyone loves an underdog.

But what does the man have to gain? He shows no courage by entering the ring with a woman. He is expected to win. If he does, his victory is shallow and unsavory. He gains no honor in beating a woman — the idea is offensive even to a modern man's vestigial sense of chivalry. Imagine the sportscaster shouting about how he "really slaughtered her." How *ignoble*!

And if he loses, the loss is so much more humiliating. While her womanhood is never in question, his masculinity is on the line. He ends up looking like a poor specimen of manhood. Women won't respect him, and men will be ashamed to be associated with him. He would be better loved by all for cheating and obviously throwing the fight, or for graciously bowing out. To give maximum effort and be bested by a woman is emasculating, no two ways about it. The same rules simply don't apply.

Apples and oranges.

Dude, you got ownd by a girl!

This all probably seems pretty obvious to most men. Somewhere deep in your left nut you know that competition with women is a net loss of honor. But I wonder if those honorable instincts are handicaps for men who, in our society, are expected to compete with women for things that matter.

When you find yourself in direct, serious competition with women, do you pull back? Do you opt out? Do you go in swinging and come out feeling depleted and ambivalent? If you agree that there is no honorable triumph over a woman — save in the bedroom or in matters of romance — how does that affect the decisions you make in life?

How do you feel when you tell a female or a feminist "what's what?" What have you gained when, in your eyes, you've won an argument with a woman? *Was it worth your time?*

"MOTHER MAY I?" MASCULINITY

Modern women balk at any suggestion that men should be able to tell women how to behave. Many believe that a woman should be able to do whatever she likes without worrying "what women are supposed to do."

When feminists talk to men, they pretend to offer the same sort of freedom from social expectations attached to one's sex. *This is always a lie.* This new, "free" model of manhood approved by feminists must, after all, serve the interests of feminism. Many traditionally masculine behaviors and ideas are clearly "off limits." So, while the new woman does whatever she wants and explores her world unfettered, the feminist male is carefully restricted and monitored for signs of disobedience or treachery.

He's a rhinestone collared lapdog with a humiliating barrette in his hair, free to run in a yard bordered by an electric fence.

At best, he's allowed the manly privileges of opening jars and taking out the garbage.

The pro-feminist male is a wretched, guilt-ridden creature who must at every turn make certain he is not impeding the progress of women in any way. He willingly accepts guilt for crimes against women he never committed, perpetrated by men he has never met. He must question any interest he has in sports or any admiration he might have for traditional male role models — for fear that he is perpetuating cultures of honor or patriarchy that could somehow result in the oppression of or violence against women. He must be careful to include women in every activity, even if he would prefer not to. He must avoid pornography. He must "Try hard to understand how [his] own attitudes and actions might inadvertently perpetuate sexism and violence, and work toward changing them."[1] He must never collude with men to work for the interests of men — unless those interests have been certified as completely harmless to the interests of women. He is encouraged to work with women to support their interests with little or no regard for how those interests might have a negative impact on men. He must "create systems of accountability to women in [his] community." He must reject any advantages he receives that seem to be tied to "systems of male privilege" but he must support and defend programs that help or give advantages to women based on their sex alone.

The only "freedom" that feminism offers men is the freedom to do exactly what women want men to do. *The freedom to serve.*

---

1   These quotations are from feminist activist Jackson Katz's "Ten Things Men Can Do To Prevent Gender Violence." http://www.jacksonkatz.com/wmcd.html

Moderate feminists sometimes make the argument that feminism is truly "humanism" and that the interests of men and women are essentially the same. This is a debatable belief — not a fact — and we must respect it, as H.L. Mencken wrote, "only in the sense and to the extent that we respect [a man's] theory that his wife is beautiful and his children smart." Men and women do share some key interests — especially when they are not in competition with one another. But so long as men and women remain physically different and demonstrate different psychological and political tendencies, some conflicts of interest between them will naturally continue.

No woman is expected to burden herself with concerns about how her words or actions might have a negative impact on men. The idea that women should serve the interests of men is explicitly anti-feminist, but the same is not true of men serving the interests of women. Serving the interests of women — possibly at the expense of your own — is required of men who support feminism.

What kind of a man must ask women "what kind of man may I be?"

Not a man, but a boy — a mere child picking flowers for a kiss on the cheek and a pat on the head.

Any assertion of his manhood hinges on the question "Mother, may I?"

If men are not supposed to tell women how women must behave, what right do women have to demand that men cater to their interests? Who are they to tell men what manhood means? Why should men accept their authority? What the Hell do women know about what it means to be a man?

A woman's commentary on the masculine experience is warped and distorted by her own interests, and should never be regarded as authoritative. If, as feminists have said, the personal is political, it is foolish to trust any woman not to filter her thoughts on men through her own experience and interests as a woman. The pose and the language of unbiased thought do not guarantee it.

These new, independent women should have no need to exploit a man's vestigial sense of chivalry. If they are truly suited to compete with men, they should be able to do so without special rules, privileges and protections. Men should not have to curb their behavior so that women can achieve. If "equality" were truly desired, men would never have to ask, "Mother, may I?"

Now, within any relationship or friendship between two people, compromise is inevitable and healthy. Every relationship is different, and a man and a woman should be able to make their private arrangements as best serves them both.

It is also true that some compromise at the public level is necessary to maintain even the most rudimentary civilization. But to ask men to radically alter their behavior to facilitate the success of complete strangers with whom they may well be in direct or indirect competition is absurd. That's not "equality" any more than asking a boxer to fight with one hand tied behind his back is a "fair fight."

And yet this is exactly what feminists ask of men.

"Hobble yourselves so that we can crawl over your backs."

Men need to reject this.

In the UK, there was recently some controversy over the formation of what looks like the most benignly pro-feminist men's therapy and health education group you could possibly imagine. But it was too much for some women to entertain the possibility that men might have any valid concerns or complaints of their own, or that they should have access to the same kinds of sex-specific support networks that now abound for women. The group's leader fell all over himself trying to justify his existence to female critics, trying to prove that he was "one of the good ones" and that his focus on masculinity wasn't a threat to women or gays or the transgendered. Perhaps this appeased his masters.

Men are doing this everywhere. They're apologizing and appeasing and asking for permission, cowering and begging and finding out that it will never, ever be enough.

Maybe some men believe that unless they hold their tongues and surrender to the never-ending demands of women, they'll never get laid again. Maybe they're afraid of being alone, unloved or scorned by women. Maybe they're afraid that if they really look into the abyss and see the situation for what it is, they'll be consumed by anger and hatred and they'll no longer be able to smile and nod their way through the crowd of oblivious and obedient consumers who are their friends, families, employers and clients. Buckin' the system ain't great for business. So men lie to themselves and pretend everything is fine to keep things on an even keel.

Damage control.
It's a little too easy for me, having little use for women and few reasons to compromise with them, to tell other men what I think they should do. So I'll just ask:

"How's that working out for ya, fellas?"

Change will begin when men stop working from willingly handicapped, defensive positions.

Men need to stop apologizing for being men.

And most of all, they need to stop asking for permission to be men.

DRAW THE LINE

What is feminism, if not refusing to exclude women from groups of men?

Feminism is branch of liberal egalitarianism. It's a lie that comes from a lie. The lie that "all men are created equal" engenders the lie that "all men and women are created equal."

Equality is a roller that flattens human social topography. There is no hierarchy — no up or down or in or out. There's nowhere to climb and nowhere to fall. Everyone is everywhere. No one is excluded. Nothing is closed. The space is open. No one and nowhere is better than any person or place. All movement is lateral.

In practical terms achieving equality between men and women is predominantly about achieving political, legal and economic equality. In practice, the success of the feminist initiative has been measured by the ability of women to infiltrate previously male spaces. There can be no separate sex roles, because everyone must be everywhere, and no one can be excluded from anything. No difference between what men do and what women do can be defined, because to define is to exclude. The doctrine of equality demands that women do whatever men do and be wherever men are.

Refusing to exclude a woman from a group of men as a matter of principal is a feminist act.

If you can't exclude a woman, you are the problem.

If you truly believe that men lose nothing of value when women are introduced to male groups — or even that all male groups are improved by female participation — you are a feminist egalitarian, and men who are not feminist egalitarians should exclude you.

I don't believe that the majority of men feel no sense of loss when they are pressured to include a woman in a male group. Most men would prefer to be able to do certain things with men, other things with women, and some things in mixed groups.

Men often convince themselves that they lose nothing by including women because they are greedy, lazy or afraid — and then attribute that revelation to a nobility of character to make themselves feel better.

If you're trying to make a profit, it's advantageous to include women whether they are wanted or not, because modern men have been conditioned to tolerate the presence of women everywhere, and excluding a woman is excluding a potential customer.

This is also why multiculturalism and globalist capitalism have become symbiotic. When everyone has a dollar sign over his or her head, exclusivity means tossing money over the moat. Including everyone makes everyone a potential customer.

Men who are selling something imagine themselves chivalrous for inviting women into male spaces because it's better than admitting that they are greedy or desperate. Principles are expensive.

The same rule applies to groups who need "support." Many nominally anti-feminist or patriarchal groups make the error of pandering to women, for fear of losing "support" — be it financial or political. Unfortunately, in doing this, those groups inevitably compromise the very principals that make them anti-feminist or patriarchal. Groups of men should follow the Roman example. When you have a power base, women are easy enough to attain — one way or another. Empty pandering is for the shoe salesmen of democracy.

Inclusion is the path of least resistance. Establishing and defending boundaries always takes work. It's easier to let lines be crossed and then rationalize your laziness after nothing can be done.

Taking a stand means taking heat. Saying "no" will have consequences. No one likes to be excluded, and when you move to exclude someone, they will lash out emotionally. You risk insult and shaming. In our feminist, egalitarian society, saying "no" to women may mean that other men will be afraid (or won't be allowed) to associate with you, for fear of being shamed themselves. When you move to exclude someone, and the prevailing morality abhors exclusion, you will be punished socially and you must accept the possibility that you may yourself be excluded. It is far easier to avoid the consequences of exclusion, and then imagine yourself a brave hero for "breaking down barriers."

You are not running an underground railroad for women.

There are no significant financial, legal or social penalties in mainstream American society associated with the inclusion of women. The only thing you risk is a pat on the head, and there is no such thing as courage without risk.

There's nothing brave about giving women whatever they ask for.

It's called "being a chump."

If you want to live in a world where men can be men and women can be women, where the sexes can have distinct roles and different meaningful identities, you have to be prepared to draw the line. If you want the men around you to be masculine and the women around you to be feminine, you have to be prepared to define the boundaries of masculinity and femininity. If the experience of brotherhood is important to you, then you can't invite sisters into every room.

Excluding women isn't the same as "hating" them.

Don't allow liberal egalitarians to define all of your terms and frame all of your arguments. Enforcing absolute equality and inclusion in everything for everyone isn't the same as love. Cultivating distinct and separate identities for different groups of people isn't the same as hate.
Refusing to give women whatever they ask for is not hate.

Human communities have always had separate spaces where men can be men and women can be women. Today, women call their separate spaces "safe spaces." Men have no sanctioned "safe spaces," though if they did, they wouldn't call them that, because wanting "safety" sounds cowardly and unmanly. Men don't need "safe" spaces. They do need their own spaces, and their own time, and their own identities. Men need spaces where they can speak freely and frankly–where they are not expected to edit their commentary to pander to the interests and agendas of women.

Creating space for men doesn't require a special government program, or a professional mediator, or a formal conference. You don't need some kind of awkward weekend retreat.

All you need is men who are willing to draw the line and hold it.

EVERYONE A HARLOT

Ego-inflating rhetoric is everywhere. At work, at school , and at the mall, Americans expect everyone to tell 'em how special, talented and important they are. In our inverted world, the weak are somehow strong, everyone who survives a hangnail is "brave," and every bean-counter who works for the Department of Defense is a goddamn hero.

At GloboCorp, the human resources department tries to convince every John and Juanita that they are absolutely essential to the success of the organization. Everyone's creative talents are valued, and everyone from the janitor to the CEO is capable of making tremendous positive contributions. In his recent book about the value of work, Matthew B. Crawford argued that modern corporations devalue meaningful achievement when they pander to us and speak as though everyone were some sort of Einstein.

Americans like to be told that they are brilliant and brave, but as a people these aren't our highest values anymore. Who can name five legitimate, recent war heroes? The hoi polloi don't care too much about who is smart, either. They only care about science when they want to lose weight, win an argument on the Internet, or find out how the world is going to end. If you can name ten guys doing hard science right now, you're probably a scientist.

Most people know they aren't Einsteins, and they really don't care. They have a more pressing concern.

What they're really asking themselves is, "Am I hot, or not?"

Beautiful people are the brightest beacons in our floating world. Attractive models and actors get far more praise and attention than Medal of Honor recipients. People love technology, but they use it to keep up with the Kardasians. They pack into gyms, but strength and fitness are by-products of their desire to be desired. A six-pack has a higher value than a powerful bench press or a heavy squat. No one cares how much Tatum Channing or Brad Pitt lifts, or how fast they can run, or what they can build, or how many men they could defeat in combat. They're admired for being desirable.

It used to be that only young women worried excessively about being desired. In traditional patriarchal societies, a woman who no one wants as a wife becomes a burden on her parents. An unwanted woman could never become a mother or run a household. She remained forever a dependent daughter or an independent, lonely spinster. For women of marriageable age, attractiveness had a very high value, and while the importance of attractiveness decreases with age, most men would still rather have a pretty wife than an ugly one. Whether by habit or by nature, many women tend to enjoy painting and adorning themselves to appear youthful, fertile, feminine and appealing.

However, the woman who cares the most about being desired is the harlot, because her survival depends on her ability to lure men into her loins.

Some will point to male ornamentation as a counter-example, but the motivation behind male embellishment has traditionally been different. When men decorated themselves, they did it to appear more fearsome or to communicate status. Samurai wore rouge, and like many finer points of samurai grooming, they did it so that their enemies would respect them as virile opponents even after they were dead. They didn't tart themselves up to get laid. They did it to gain the respect of men.

Last weekend, a movie about male strippers made $39.2 million dollars at the box office. America's come a long way since *Flashdance*.

In *The Way of Men*, I used Bonobos and Chimpanzees to compare the female-oriented society to the male-oriented society. People aren't exactly the same as apes, but I think Chimps and Bonobos make revealing metaphors for where we've been, and where we seem to be headed.

Bonobos live luxuriously, with access to as much food as they need. Female coalitions check male aggression, and males rarely form tight-knit groups. Males don't know who their fathers are, only their mothers. Sex is, as a bar whore once said to a pal of mine, "like shaking hands." Homosexuality is commonplace because sex is a social activity, and everyone has sex with everyone. It's not about reproduction; sex is about mutual masturbation and having a good time. Sex is a major part of bonobo life. Bonobos are said to be peaceful, and while that may not be completely true, they're definitely matrilineal and exceptionally horny.

Chimpanzees form patriarchal hunting groups. The males stick together, and the females end up moving from group to group. Sex is a reproductive activity. Homosexuality is rare. Males dominate females and the males at the top of the male hierarchy control the group.

America is fast becoming a "Bonobo Masturbation Society," devoted to pleasure and organized primarily to serve the interests of females. More and more men are raised by single mothers, and males are discouraged from organizing without female supervision. Sex is social, and the majority of the hard, dangerous work that men used to do is either done by machines, idiot-proofed, or outsourced to countries where life is cheap. Women and dishonorable men micromanage male aggression with endless laws and lawsuits, and bad boys who can't pay big lawyers are drop-kicked into a multi-billion dollar prison industry that boasts the highest incarceration rate in the world.

In our Bonobo Masturbation Society, fucking is one of the only things men are encouraged to do that actually makes them feel like men.

Throughout the Alt-Right, several writers have criticized "pick-up artist" culture and "game."

I am more sympathetic, because banging is just about the only manly thing most men are allowed to do. I see what many call game as a kind of gateway masculinity. Game is essentially assertiveness training for a generation of young men who spent most of their lives playing "mother may I?"

Manliness is like a talent. Some males are more gifted than others, but like any talent, masculinity has to be pushed and developed to amount to anything impressive. Boys who were raised by single moms or overprotective parents and put through the public school feminist brain-washing system were never tried or trained by groups of hard men. You can't hand a hen-pecked boy a high school diploma and expect him to spit like Clint Eastwood.

When they talk about game, men in the "manosphere" are shoveling through the bullshit that the system tells boys about girls. This is work that needs to be done. If average young guys believe the official malarkey they are told about sex and relationships, they'll be used and abused by entitled American girls for the rest of their lives. And, as they un-pack feminist myths about the sexes, I've seen a lot of those guys start to wonder what it really means to be men. This is an important conversation. However, it almost seems like a safer route in today's cultural climate to make chasing poon a long-term lifestyle choice. That's where the positive mean slides toward a negative extreme.

Andy Nowicki wrote that if men really wanted to undermine the matriarchy, they would stop fucking. He may have his own (possibly religious) reasons for saying so, but I think he has a point.

Our feminist, globalist handlers would love nothing more than to keep young men — the most dangerous and potentially revolutionary group in any civilization – completely distracted by tang. And while it may feel like asserting dominance (in conveniently the most harmless way possible), if everything you do is designed to make you more appealing to women, you're an eager vibrator. When your muscle is just for show, when everything you do is to make yourself more desirable, you're playing the female role. When your worth as a man depends on how many women you can lure to your loins, you're just a gigolo.

As Hunter S. Thompson noted, sex is the most fun for amateurs. It's great when you're young, pretty, naïve and carefree — but "old whores don't do much giggling."

Mark Simpson had a lot of this figured out when he coined the word "metrosexual" way back in 1994. The metrosexual is not necessarily gay or effeminate in the flamboyant sense of the word — that's just the way people picked up the word. Simpson's idea of the metrosexual is a "mirror man" whose highest narcissistic concerns are pleasure-seeking and being regarded as "desirable." He may be in love with himself, but that, too, is a shallow kind of love. He cares more about how he looks and how well he fucks than what he has achieved or how well he is respected. It's a harlot's vanity.

Hugh Hefner was far ahead of his time. It was homosexual men who pioneered the bonobo lifestyle en masse. Before today's PUAs were in pre-school, homos were doing it for the numbers, looking for validation, basing their self-worth on how many and how hot. Homosexual men rejected traditional male roles and expectations, and channeled all of their masculine aggression into sex for the sake of sex. Their idea of masculinity became masturbatory — a pumped up Tom of Finland caricature of masculine form without function or honor or virtue. Homosexual men, because they were men, set the cultural stage for objectifying men the way that men have always objectified women.

As pilot bonobos, the homos discovered the downsides of harlotry. An experienced player was bound to acquire a handful of STDs, and AIDS practically wiped out an entire generation of "sexually liberated" men. For many, there are also psychological costs. Being desired is a drug, and it's addictive. When it's your highest value, it becomes your identity. One of the problems — and this has always been a curse to women — is that sexual attractiveness is linked to the mating instinct, and it peaks in the young. Men mature more flatteringly than women, but most men who trade on their sex appeal won't relax into the confident, secure, middle-aged manhood of their forefathers. Like homos and movie stars, I wonder how many of today's players will chase steroids and sex drugs and eventually convince themselves that maybe that Kenny Rogers face lift will look better on them than it does on him. (It won't, fellas. You'll still look like an old lesbian who can't blink.) There's something particularly desperate, sad and undignified about a man of a certain age who spends too much time looking for sexual validation.

What's worse is that straight men aren't in the market for men, they're in the market for women, so biology puts them at a major disadvantage. Game strategist Heartiste once posted about an online dating experiment where together, the two best looking guys managed to get a total of 50 messages from women, while the most attractive woman got over 536 messages from men in the same time period. That playing field will never be close to equal, but game is gaining popularity because men see that disparity and want to increase their odds.

Good-looking men with some game may be able to keep at it for most of their lives, and they'll end up with some good stories. A small minority of men have always been libertines, and some men are probably particularly well suited to it. Some will have regrets, and some won't.

The problem isn't what happens to a few players, but what we become as a society when everyone wants to be a player. Libertinism used to be a form of rebellion, but increasingly, it's part of the program. In a society where sex and attractiveness are the highest values, what happens to the other two-thirds of the curve?

The flesh won't be democratized. Attractiveness isn't any more evenly distributed than strength, size, or IQ. The world is full of fat, ugly people. People can improve their lot with diet and exercise and grooming — and they should — but you can only put so much lipstick on a pig. Some men and women just aren't that great looking. A lot of people are actually pretty repulsive. A few should probably avoid daylight altogether, because they frighten small children.

Women have always been aware of the cruel elitism of beauty's natural hierarchy. In societies where other virtues had higher value, they could focus on piety or simply being good mothers. When women were "sexually liberated," some feminists (usually the fat, ugly ones) thought they could rely on social conditioning to give us all permanent beer goggles and make every bloated hag as desirable as Heather Locklear. If only Barbie had realistic proportions, or we were forced to watch more morbidly obese people on television, then fewer tears would tumble into buckets of ice cream. They keep pushing for "fat acceptance" and keep telling us that "big is beautiful." When that doesn't work, they barrage us with bad clichés and try to convince us that beauty is either in the eye of the beholder, or "on the inside." We might patronize them, or try to be more sensitive, but pretending everyone is equally beautiful is just as absurd and untrue as pretending everyone is an Einstein.

No one wants a Barbie doll with cankles, and the de-objectification of women is at odds with the Zeitgeist of our oversexed Bonobo Masturbation Society. Andrea Dworkin lost, and more teenage girls than ever are watching hardcore porn to learn how to twist, stroke and swallow like the pros. I go to the gym and I see young guys who aren't there to lift or get big. They're following routines to "cut up" and build a body "for the ladies." Those ladies are tanning, getting boob jobs, and trying to look like strippers. A friend who teaches at a high school in California said they had to cancel Halloween dress-up days because the kids didn't want to be scary or cute anymore. Boys and girls alike used the holiday as an excuse to come to school as close to naked as possible.

People used to have decent aspirations. They wanted to have families. They wanted to do good work. They wanted to be good citizens, good Christians, good people. Now everyone wants to be a player and a porn star. Everyone wants to be the kind of monkey that all of the other monkeys wants to rub up against.

We call this matrilineal hump-fest "progress," and seek our moral redemption in recycling.

Sex may be natural, and it sure is fun, but it's just a part of life. A society that over-emphasizes sex to the point where it seems like the only thing in life that means anything is grotesque and degraded, and for most people it delivers more emptiness than ecstasy.

In healthy patriarchies, men push themselves to earn the respect and admiration of other men. They work to prove their strength, courage and competence to each other. Men pride themselves on their reputation for mastery of their bodies, their actions, and their environment. They want to be known for what they can do, not just how well or who they can screw. And they sure as hell don't waste their time trying to figure out what they can do to bedazzle bimbos.

Hell, in some places, when a man is ready to take a wife, he just picks one andkidnaps her. Men used to get married and get on with their lives. It seems like a healthier life path to me, and I've previewed what the other side has to offer.

Recently, I watched *Restrepo*, a documentary about soldiers fighting in Afghanistan. There was this scene in it where the Americans had to negotiate with local tribal elders. The elders were a bunch of dead serious-looking old dudes and their long beards were dyed bright red with henna.

Our tribal "allies" in the graveyard of empires have their problems. They shit in their hands and rape little boys. Their customs leave room for improvement.

However, as I watched their grave eyes, I wondered if any of these men had spent much time wondering, "Am I hot, or not?"

TRAIN FOR HONOR

The phrase "survival of the fittest" was coined by Herbert Spencer, a contemporary of Charles Darwin. In Darwinian terms, the living thing that is "fit" is well-adapted to survive in its environment, and the "unfit" thing is poorly adapted to its environment — *a fish out of water,* so to speak. The thing that survives — because it is "fit enough" — lives to reproduce and pass on its genes to the next generation.

Being "physically fit" doesn't mean being the biggest or the fastest or the strongest. The tiny bee may be just as well adapted to its immediate environment as the mighty bear. Both are "fit enough."

Our primal fathers didn't "work out" to stay "physically fit."

To survive in the wild, they had to lift and carry and run. They had to hunt and work to gather food. They had to fight off animals and other groups of men. Our species adapted to this harder way of life.

Men today can train their bodies to do a tremendous amount

of physical work — be it distance running or heavy lifting — because our ancestors sometimes needed to do Herculean things to survive. I doubt the average caveman ever had to squat 800 pounds, but men today can do it by manipulating the physical systems, processes and potentials that developed to survive in a more far demanding natural environment.

What does it mean, then, to be "physically fit" today?

In modern, First World countries, a man can live his whole life without any kind of physical exertion. Actually, physical exertion is relative, because the weaker you are, the lower the point is where movement becomes "exertion." Some men have to exert themselves to get off the couch. But even those men are "fit enough." By some miracle, they routinely manage to huff and puff and dribble their seed into some cow who will then birth the next generation of indolent ball scratchers.

Being "fit enough" for the modern environment simply means being able to roll yourself from your bed to a vehicle and drive to a job where you sit in a chair, tap on a keyboard for a while, then lumber back to the vehicle and pick up some fast food from a drive-through window on the way back to your bed. If you get too fat or too weak to do that, you can probably collect welfare and have someone deliver your food.

Even if you're a real go-getter, you never have to be very strong. The average man never has to be stronger than the average woman or even the pre-teen girl. If you eat healthy foods and manage your diet well, you will be "fit enough" to meet the physical demands of most prestigious jobs and you will probably live a relatively long life. That's "fit enough."

So why "work out?"

Why spend hours in a gym, lifting or training to perform feats that you will never really need to perform to survive?

I'm a writer and an artist. I could write more books and make more art if I stopped spending an average of 6 to 10 hours a week working out. That's an entire work day of lost time every week. If I work out 8 hours a week for 50 years, that's almost 2 ½ years of my life in spent the gym. I'm not a professional athlete. No one cares how much I can lift. No one cares how fast or far I can run. I'm not a soldier. I *could* carry a grown man on my back for a mile, but I will probably never *have* to.

My works are my progeny. My books and essays and images and ideas are what I send out into the world. Whatever impact they make on others is the only part of me that will survive my death.

My body is a depreciating asset. My body is temporary, and no matter what I do, it will eventually fail and fall apart and become worthless. Why put so much into something that is dying?

Whatever you do, you could probably do more of it if you didn't spend so much time maintaining or attempting to improve parts of your dying body.

Why bother?

Given the investment of time and the potential loss of productivity, I think it's important to think about your motivation. What reasons can justify working to become physically stronger or faster or more agile or more skillful than necessary to be "fit enough" to survive in the modern environment?

One could argue that the modern, First World lifestyle is unsustainable. As any evolutionary biologist would point out, environments change, and part of being "fit enough" also means being able to survive potential changes to your environment. It's naive to assume that things will always be as they are now. What we know as the First World way of life was the result of phenomenal growth and excess in the 20th Century. That's a blip in human history. Due to limited resources — *due to limited space on Earth* — that kind of endless growth is impossible to maintain. When this complex civilization collapses, men will need to be stronger than teenage girls again.

Training to be prepared for harder times is valid. It's a good enough reason to train — a *manly* reason.

I'm going to put that aside.

Why would you train *anyway*?

Why would you train if you weren't expecting doomsday at any moment?

Why would it be worth training even if you never live to see your strength needed to survive?

It's a question I think a man should have an good answer to if he's going to put aside other tasks and force himself to train 3 to 6 days a week for the rest of his life.

A man should have a manly answer to this question, and I think finding the right answer — an answer you can be proud of — can provide the motivation you need to keep training.

We are told that we're supposed to work out to stay healthy. This is why the "experts" on TV and in the government tell us to exercise — in moderation. Good citizens need to stay just healthy enough to get around unassisted, so that they can keep filing their paperwork and keep paying their bills and keep buying things.

People who are in reasonably good health are more functional all around, and less of a burden on those around them. That's better than nothing.

But living "longer and happier" is a mediocre and uninspiring reason to get up and go to the gym every day. It reduces training your own body to bourgeois busywork, like mowing the lawn or doing the laundry. There is no manly exploit or display of prowess in mere "health maintenance" — only the repetitive execution of menial processes. This is probably why less ambitious amateur exercisers bitch and moan about going to the gym. For them, it's just another chore.

The majority of men — men who aren't athletes or cops or soldiers or firefighters — work out because they want to look good. Most men today train to be attractive.

This overcivilized "Bonobo Masturbation Society" prohibits or highly regulates opportunities for men to display Strength, Courage, Mastery and Honor. Sexual domination is one of the only acceptable ways that men can feel like men, so displaying sexual mastery has increased in value. Hypersexualization is promoted through pornography and the media, so more men want to look and feel like porn stars.

As the relative cultural importance of sex increases and women become more financially independent, more heterosexual men are getting a taste of the kind of power that women have always had — the power of sexual selection. Some physically attractive men seem to be able to have any girl they want. Gyms are full of young guys doing bicep curls and crunches "for the ladies," because they want to be *that guy*, or at least increase their range of options by making themselves more attractive.

It's better to be attractive than it is to be unattractive, and everyone would rather be desirable than undesirable. No one *wants* to be Quasimodo. Everyone wants to be wanted. This is human nature, and is to be expected.

However, as a primary or sole motivator, "looking good" is a harlotrous reason to work out. It's basically saying that you spend hours every week trying to stay pretty. Being man-pretty may mean having big guns, a nice rack and a six-pack, but if you're only building that body to be "hot," then you're basically no different than the strippers and aspiring trophy wives and go-girl cocktail sluts who are doing the same thing. Striving only to be desired is passive and effeminate.

An attractive body may look very manly — and may even be quite strong — but trying to stay "hot" is a desperate reason for a grown man to spend hours and days and years at the gym if it's the only reason.

This also a problem with bodybuilding.

When I'm trying to determine if a thing is manly or un-manly, I look to the end of it. The end of bodybuilding as a concept is purely aesthetic. While sculpting the physique of a fitness model or amatuer bodybuilder requires incedible mastery and extreme self-discipline, the ultimate goal is to achieve a certain "look." In bodybuilding, actual strength is a by-product of pursuing the *appearance* of strength. How much a bodybuilder can lift is less important to him than how much he looks like he can lift.

Lifting for strength, power and performance is conceptually manlier than lifting for aesthetics alone. Many powerlifters look physically less impressive — less obviously muscular — than bodybuilders, but they can perform amazing feats of strength. I train off and on at a powerlifting gym, and I regularly see guys who don't look very strong at all deadlifting or squatting well over 500 pounds.

The end of powerlifting, strongman training and any kind of training to improve performance in a sporting event is the pursuit of Strength, one of the tactical virtues of masculinity.

Training for Strength — or to increase any kind of athletic ability — is admirable. It's a masculine pursuit. It's fundamentally about action and achievement, not merely appearances.

Still, though, there's the problem of strength "for what?"

Strength does have its advantages.

I like being reasonably strong, and as I get older and the men of my generation get softer, I like being stronger than most other men my age. I know that it isn't saying much, and it speaks more to their weakness than to my strength, but it's something. You don't have to be strong in the modern world, but strength is always useful, and it is still better to be strong than it is to be weak. Tasks that are difficult for other people are easy for me. I am a more useful and less dependent man because I train, and this is good. I train to be fitter than "fit enough."

While bodybuilding for purely aesthetic reasons is problematic from a masculine perspective, it is also true that the appearance of strength has certain tactical advantages.

Martial arts training is the manliest kind of training, because its end is directly related to the primal role of men — fighting and defending.

However, training in the martial arts doesn't necessarily

make you appear to be formidable.

Training to *look* formidable is an aesthetic pursuit with a tactical end. Because it is concerned with appearances, it is often confused with training for attractiveness, but there's a huge conceptual difference between training to *scare* men and training to *attract* women.

"Threat display" is a masculine end for bodybuilding, and a reason to incorporate bodybuilding methods and movements into training.

I'm no juggernaut, but no matter how much I can lift or what I can actually do, I've noticed that men respond to me differently when I look stronger. I've had many male co-workers and associates speculate aloud (and unprompted) about how I could probably kick their asses, based mostly on the size of my arms. Arm size probably doesn't have much to do with fighting ability, but it's something other men notice when they evaluate you as a threat — especially if they don't even lift. Sometimes being bigger lets you roll into a male social group as the default "alpha" without even doing or saying much of anything.

A friend of mine who works occasionally as a bouncer once explained to me that being bigger and more physically intimidating has allowed him to resolve conflicts *without* having to fight.

Naturally, this leads to escalation. Because bodybuilding has become part of modern culture. Many men get bigger than they would be from simply doing hard labor, so to create the same kind of threat display, you have to train to be as big or bigger than they are to have the same social and tactical advantage.

It is foolish, however, to confuse looking like a badass with actually *being* a badass.

A man can train to attract women, but men will admire him more if he trains to scare other men. A man can train to improve or maintain his health, but training to perform feats of strength, speed or skill is more virile, more motivating, and ultimately more satisfying. A man can train for self-defense, to be more self-reliant, to be ready to fight in the event of an emergency where the agents of law and order become unable or unwilling to protect and serve the people he cares about most. All of these reasons are good enough reasons to train — they are reasons as good or better than the reasons people give for doing *anything* they don't have to do in the modern world. Each is somewhat masturbatory, but almost everything is masturbatory in a spoiled world where exertion and strife are simulations or self-created dramas — luxuries and indulgences — because they are divorced from the animal urgencies of hunger and danger. Almost *everything* you do in your safe, suburban middle class home is in some sense masturbatory, self-indulgent, unnecessary and utterly pointless. But we are alive now and we live in this place and time, so the best we can do is make the best approximations of the lives we believe to be best. The best we can do is act and behave "as if."

Acting and behaving "as if" brings me to the conclusion I finally reached in my own search for a higher, better reason for spending so many hours of my life in the gym, maintaining and improving my dying body.

I train for honor.

I train because I refuse to be a soft ambassador of this Age of Atrophy. And I refuse to be shuffling, slobbering, potato chip gobbling evidence of modern decay.

I refuse to be "Exhibit A."

I understand that it has become socially acceptable, even fashionable, for men to be slender and delicate. I know that to demand more of a man like that is considered bullying — or "homophobia." Magazines and advertisements are full of photos of men in pink dress shirts with breakable-looking arms and absent shoulders. Government health sources tell us we should watch our "BMI" (Body Mass Index), which considers only height and weight and penalizes muscle mass. Strong men are considered "overweight" or "obese." I would have to lose 100% of my bodyfat and a pound or two of muscle to weigh what the Center for Disease Control considers "normal" for my height.

If honor has to do with a man's reputation among his male peers, then there is no dishonor in weakness by contemporary standards. An exceptionally weak man can easily find a group of frail men to accept and affirm his weakness.

I also understand that, while the State officially discourages obesity, there are entire communities whose failing infrastructures creak under the grotesque girth of men who cannot see their feet — much less their dicks — when standing upright. Boyish frailty may be the new "normal" for educated urbanites, but the true American norm is swollen, doughy, diabetic corpulence.

So, if honor has to do with a man's reputation among his male peers, then there is no dishonor in obesity by contemporary American standards. Any blubbery fat man who can barely walk can easily find a drove of pigs to accept and affirm his fatness.

It is true that I could be fat and weak and still gain the respect and admiration of average men. If I never set foot in a gym again I could be "fit enough" for the majority of my male peers. There is no dishonor in that today. But *there should be.*

The athletic potential of the male body is wasted on the modern world. The best of us occupy ourselves by training to perform tricks and play games, but our bodies are built for work and for action. Men are capable of Herculean labors, and the male machine wants, at the apex of its potential, to be hurled in a warp spasm of muscular inertia at danger and, ultimately, death.

I don't train to be "fit enough" for the modern world, or to gain the esteem of the average modern man. I train because somewhere in my DNA there's a memory of a more ferocious world, a world where men could become what they are and reach the most terrifyingly magnificent state of their nature. I don't train to impress the majority of modern slobs. I train to be worthy enough to *carry water* for my barbarian fathers, and to be worthy of the company of the men most like them alive today. I train because I imagine the disgust and contempt our ancestors would have for us all if they lined up modern men on the street. I train to be less of an embarrassment to their memory. I train because most modern men dishonor all of the men who came before them. I train "as if" they were watching and judging us. I train "as if" I might one day be called to join them, or to strive and thrive as they once did, in a better world — a greater age. I train because it is better to imagine oneself as a soldier in a spiritual army training for a war that may never come than it is to shrug, slouch and shuffle forward into a dysgenic and dystopian future.

Honor is a higher reason to train, a higher cause, a motivation above and beyond the routine and mundane. It's a better reason to keep going to the gym than mere narcissism or the fear of immobility, impotence and death. I admit that I still train for all of the other reasons that other men train. I'm just as much a product of modernity as anyone else. But when I need a better reason to train — because I know I don't have to train, and that people will still accept and respect me whether I train or not — I train for honor.

THE PHYSICAL CHALLENGE

"May you live long," the old man said.

I looked over my shoulder. Some old timer had followed me up the stairs. I wasn't sure if he belonged in the building, or if he had just walked in off the street.

"I think you're the last man in America doin' work like that."

"I might be."

Every Saturday for the last 9 months it's been my job to deliver a palette of grain to a downtown brewery. I counted the bags yesterday. 44 bags of grain, 50 pounds each. It varies from week to week, but that's a pretty standard load. The brewery is on the mezzanine, up 2 flights of about 10 stairs. There is an elevator.

All of the drivers bitch about doing the grain. It's some sweetheart deal my company has worked out with a local brewery chain. We charge 'em 50 bucks. I make 12 an hour. I'm off Sundays and Mondays, so it's the last thing I have to do before my weekend starts.

The standard technique is to put the truck's ramp down and load up 4-5 bags on a board, then pick up the stack with one of our piece-of-shit handtrucks and wheel it down the ramp and into the building. Downstack; repeat. Takes about an hour—that's 12 bucks, before taxes—and it's a pain in the ass no matter what. Bags of grain don't like to stay on hand trucks. If you don't stack 'em just right, the stack falls down and you have to do it all over again. If I got paid more, I would buy a better handtruck or build a better board. It should be easier. I could probably do all of the grain stops for the whole company in one day if I rigged it right, but it's an old company and they aren't into reinventing the wheel. They've been doing it this way for at least a decade. I've had over 35 jobs, and some companies are less amenable to innovation than others. You get a feel for which ones are which.

I actually *like* hard work. I prefer it over lying.

I'm broken like that.

When it started to rain this year, I realized I wouldn't be able to make it down the ramp with an 8-stack without a high risk of slipping. Then it struck me.

I wondered if I could carry the whole load upstairs on my shoulder, two bags at a time. I was pretty sure I could. I decided to give it a try and see if it was time effective. I figured it would be a pretty good workout and save me a trip to the gym on my Friday night.

I downstacked a row of bags onto the tail, bear-hugged two bags and then popped them onto my shoulder with a hip thrust. Solid enough. Guy at the front desk looked confused when I went for the stairs.

22 trips. 2 flights of stairs. 100 pounds on my shoulder. Plus downstacking. Sometimes in the heat. Sometimes in the rain. Sometimes I have to park up the block. That's when it really hurts.

The first time I did it, I felt superhuman. It was like a Herculean labor.

Truth is, it's not superhuman.

Any healthy guy my size *should* be able to do this. I'm not special. A few generations ago, the smaller, harder men who built this country probably broke their backs doing shit like this every day. This is the kind of hard work that built castles and bridges and railroads.

Today, many men my size couldn't, and most that could -- wouldn't.
They think they're too good for it, too smart for it. The embalmed "health experts" on TV tell them they might hurt their precious backs.

Gods forbid.

Some of the guys who see me doing it probably think I'm crazy. Most probably think I'm stupid, like I didn't *realize* it could be done with a hand truck or a cart or something that would make it easier. But every so often one of them, like the old guy, appreciates the fact that I am doing *work*.

When I'm working, I think of all the people in the gym paying personal trainers 60 bucks an hour to make them do squats with a 12 pound Nike medicine ball. I think of all the people on Stairmasters carrying nothing. I think of the fitness gurus selling sandbags for 120 dollars (plus shipping and handling). I think of all the schmucks doing lateral raises on Bosu balls to "activate" their "cores."

"Working out" is a substitute for work. It's forcing your body to do what it wants to do, what it's made to do. Modern life provides fewer and fewer opportunities to do real work. Hard work.

Here's some fitness advice for you:

The next time you have the opportunity to do real work, take it. *Take the physical challenge.* Do the work. Don't try to make it *easier* so you can work "smarter."

Try working *harder*.

It's amazing how much carrying heavy shit up stairs "activates" your "core."

Think about that for me the next time you take the elevator to the Stairmaster.

PRINCIPLES
OF CONVENIENCE

Your personal shortcomings and natural talents are not moral triumphs.

When I read about someone preaching sexual abstinence, I want to see what that person looks like. I don't want to be lectured about the virtues of chastity by someone who would obviously have trouble getting laid. I'm not impressed with the self-discipline or moral fortitude of an obese neckbeard or pimply teenager, and it's hard to admire the fidelity of some awkward beta who clearly married the first mediocre woman who would sleep with him for fear that he'd never find another.

Yeah, sure, buddy, it's all about your commitment to God, or to your spiritual refinement, or whatever.

You can rail all you want about the vulgar undulations of the debauched modern masses, and I'd probably agree with you, but it's a little too convenient that you, with your relatively limited options, have become a beacon of moral superiority.

If Tim Tebow is actually still a virgin, now that would be something.

This applies to many things.

I'm not impressed when ectomorphs criticize fat people for eating too much.

You can eat whatever you want and never get fat. You aren't thin because you're more disciplined — you're thin because you're lucky.

I'm not impressed when people brag about the achievements of their ancestors.

Great story. What have YOU done to be worthy of that heritage?

I'm impressed by the overcoming, by will, of adversity — not the easy righteousness of those who took the path of least resistance.

That reeks of *ressentiment*, of trying to remake the world in your own flawed image, rather than trying to remake yourself in the image of virtue.

Overcoming is not necessary — one can simply live well according to one's nature. But when you start accusing others of moral failures and transgressions, and hold yourself up as an exemplar, your opinion carries a lot more weight in my book if you've overcome the temptations you've warned against. If not — if you're just doing what you wanted to do anyway, or doing what came easiest to you — you're just bragging. Bragging is the habit of unproven men, of men who are just trying to convince you they belong one step up from the bottom of the totem pole.

Meaningful achievements are the little bullet points in life that save you from having to brag about your natural advantages, or try to trick people into believing that you are better than they are for having achieved nothing — or for having more disadvantages. It is overcoming your natural disadvantages, or working hard to develop your natural advantages, that is noteworthy and inspiring.

In every self-righteous rant, I look for the man who has overcome nothing, trying to remake the world in his own image, to save him from the trouble of remaking himself.

There are choices I have made in my life that were based on principle, and they were anything but convenient. Doing what you think is right is only worthy of admiration when the right choice isn't the easy choice. It's easy to go with the flow and adapt your moral code to whatever feels good at the time. That's the bourgeois way, the way of the merchant who becomes whoever his customers want him to be. It's the modern way, the way of lonely people with few meaningful connections, floating through this global economy, seeking temporary pleasure and instant affirmation.

I don't have much respect for principles of convenience. If you commit yourself to a way of life, if you say you stand up for a set of principles, that doesn't mean anything unless you're willing to stand up for them whether they are convenient or not.

Meaningful principles are rarely convenient in the long run.

THE MANLY BARBARIAN
Masculinity & Exploit in Veblen's
Theory of the Leisure Class

Thorstein Veblen's *Theory of the Leisure Class* was written as a treatise on economics, but in pieces—like the work of Freud and Darwin—it reads today like an early stab at evolutionary psychology. I decided to dig into it after reading Venkatesh Rao's brilliant essay "The Return of the Barbarian."[1] Rao updated some of Veblen's basic ideas and used them as a jumping off point for an argument about conflicts between sedentary cultures (which invest everything into civilization and become completely dependent on it) and pastoral nomads (who are used to thinking on their feet). I was interested in the way that the traits Veblen assigned to Barbarians overlap with the archetypal essence of masculinity I developed in *The Way of Men*. "Manliness-as-barbarianism" offers a muscular <u>way to expand </u>an anti-modern, extra-Christian understand-

1   Rao, Venkatesh. *Ribbonfarm.com.* "The Return of the Barbarian." 2011.
http://www.ribbonfarm.com/2011/03/10/the-return-of-the-barbarian/

ing of men and masculinity.

Veblen's opening "Introductory" essay is alive, colorfully written and packed with interesting ideas. The rest of the book, although peppered with smart and timeless observations, suffers from a middle class bookworm's ressentiment toward both "delinquent" bullies and predatory elitists (who he thinks have a lot in common) as well as a lot of rambling, convoluted writing and thinking about classes which no longer exist in quite the same forms.

His basic theory rests on the idea that humans were once relatively peaceful savages who acquired a predatory habit. These peaceful savages—"noble savages," you might say—shared work and resources, and could afford no class of individuals who abstained from certain kinds of work. However, as men developed the knack for preying on other living creatures, including other groups of men, divisions of labor occurred. Men are generally better suited to hunting and fighting, so hunting and fighting became man's work, and women were left to do the work which remained. This gendered split of labor occurs at the "lower" stage of barbarism, when technology has advanced to the point where hunting and fighting are feasible, and opportunities for hunting and fighting occur with enough regularity for the action to become culturally important to the group. For instance, an isolated island with plenty of fresh fruits and vegetables, but no pigs to hunt, would be less conducive to the predatory "habit" of mind.

According to Veblen, the barbarian man's work is characterized by exploit. He "reaps what he has not strewn." The manly barbarian takes what he wants with a violent hand and an iron will.

More broadly, the work of men deals with animate phenomena. Veblen stresses that, to the barbarian, that which is "animate" is not merely what is "alive." Like his contemporary Thomas Carlyle, he recognized that our forefathers inhabited a far more magical world. As Carlyle wrote in *Heroes and Hero-Worship*:

> "To the wild, deep-hearted man all was yet new, not veiled under names or formulas; it stood naked, flashing in on him there, beautiful, awful, unspeakable...
>
> ... The world, which is now divine only to the gifted, was then divine to whosoever would turn his eye upon it.[2]"

The angry volcano, the changeable sea, the exclamatory thunderclap and the snap of lighting—each one as animated as a bear or a snake or a herd of aurochs. Before our age of conceit, the whole world was alive in a way. The task of man was to challenge and master the world, to dare and to fight against its untamed fury. To leap a crevasse, to climb a mountain, to tramp through the white powder that falls from the sky. In Veblen's words, the work of men was work that demanded "prowess," not mere "diligence" and "drudgery."

According to him, "virtually the whole range of industrial employments is an outgrowth of what is classed as women's

2   Carlyle, Thomas. *On Heroes and Hero-Worship and the Heroic in History.* "Lecture I: The Hero as Divinity." University of Nebraska Press. 1966. (Page 7-9.)

work in the primitive barbarian community." Men reserved their strength for dynamic activities. Mere chores—the preparation of food, the production of clothing, the repetitive execution of menial processes—were assigned to women, to the weak and infirm, to slaves.

Masculinity must be proved, and the work that demonstrates strength, courage and mastery, bestows proof. A fresh carcass, a rack of antlers, a string of ears, your enemy's wife. These proofs of exploit convey achievement and status. The trophy is physical evidence of honor and successful initiation into the hierarchy of men, a symbolic representation of dominance demonstrated in conflict with men or beasts. Veblen wrote:

> "Under this common-sense barbarian appreciation of worth or honor, the taking of life—the killing of formidable competitors, whether brute or human—is honorable in the highest degree. And this high office of slaughter, as an expression of the slayer's prepotence, casts a glamour of worth over every act of slaughter and over all of the tools and accessories of the act. Arms are honorable, and the use of them, even in seeking the life of the meanest creatures of the fields, becomes an honorific employment. At the same time, employment in industry becomes correspondingly odious, and, in the common-sense apprehension, the handling of the tools and implements of industry falls beneath the dignity of able-bodied men. Labor becomes irksome."

The accumulation of objects of honor becomes an end in itself, and Veblen's economic theory is based on the idea that as civilizations become more complex, symbols and the appearance of honor become more important than honorific deeds themselves. The upper classes make ostentatious and often wasteful displays of wealth as a matter of habit, and—especially in the open-caste system of American society—the lower and middle classes toil to gain honor by attaining high-end goods. Hence, the popular obsession with logos, luxury vehicles and all our sundry forms of bling and swag.

More relevant to the discussion of masculinity, however, is Veblen's breakdown of manly and unmanly work. As the drudgery of industry among those engaged in lackluster occupations increases in efficiency, a surplus of goods allows particularly talented or well-born men to devote themselves completely to tasks which produce little of tangible value, but which deal specifically with the animate world and the application or management of exploit. These non-industrial occupations include government, warfare, religious observances, and sports. In the barbarian world, where manly exploit is righteousness, the highest status men are warriors, priests, and kings. Athletics include abstract rehearsals for war and the practice or demonstration of skills applicable to hunting, fighting or mastering nature. The rightful role of the barbarian priest—as storyteller, shaman, philosopher, scribe and artist—is to place the exploits of men in the magical, animate world. The barbarian priest provides the barbarian warrior with a compelling narrative. As Mishima might say, the priest finds the poetry in the splash of blood.

Veblen's take on the predatory culture of barbarian thugs—and evidence of it in the aristocracy of his time—was somewhat snide. He was clearly biased in favor of the sensible, hard-working middle class, who he saw as being less concerned with violence and exploit, and more in touch with the peaceful ways of pre-barbarian savages. Today, there is every reason to believe that tribal violence has always been golden to males, as it is even in our close ancestors, the chimpanzees. The supposedly non-violent savages studied by the scientists and explorers of Veblen's era are more reasonably understood as culs-de-sac in human cultural development. In zero scarcity pockets of peace and plenty, men tend to lapse into softness and mother-worship. Men who are attracted to the barbarian way of life—or the idea of it—continually warn against this tendency. Settled as we are in this suburban bonobo cul-de-sac of a global empire, the majority of modern men can only daydream about an age of blood and poetry, and listen to stories about the days of high adventure.

If we put aside fantasies of noble savages and recognize the barbarian as the father of all men, his interest in exploit and preference for demonstrations of prowess over mere industry help to explain some of the conflicts between manliness and our modern industrial (and post-industrial) way of life. Anti-modern passions in men, while often couched in talk of the greatness of dying or past civilizations, are also often connected to a yearning for a return to the "barbarian values" of blood, honor, magic, poetry, adventure and exploit which are forbidden to all but a few in our "evolved" modern world.

BECOMING
THE NEW BARBARIANS

This speech was delivered at the second National Policy Institute (NPI) conference, held at the Ronald Reagan Building in Washington, DC, on October 26th.

There may be a collapse.

It could happen.

It could happen tomorrow.

Vengeful gods could hurl boulders from the sky, cleansing the earth with fires and floods. There could be blood in the streets and gnashing of teeth. A plague of locusts or killer bees, some Chinese flu, or the Zombie Apocalypse.

Your debit cards might run empty and your "smart"phones might get real dumb.

We may be forced to band together in primal gangs and fight for survival. We may be forced by circumstances beyond our

control to rediscover lifeways more familiar to our species—
to our ancestral brains—than this endless, banal sprawl of
corporate parks and shopping malls.

Or you may just get that one day as a lion, to die like you were
born, kicking and screaming and covered in someone else's
blood.

It has a certain appeal.

But while any or all of that could happen (and it could all
happen tomorrow), it is also possible that this broken, corrupt system could limp along for a very long time.

Yes, it should fail catastrophically. It deserves to fail. But no
matter how much the world needs a reckoning or a reset but-
ton, it's a lot easier on a day-to-day basis for people at every
level of society to keep patching it together and doing the
best they can until they run out of duct tape.

So . . . until that day comes . . . until everyone runs out of duct
tape . . . Until then, almost everyone, even American leaders,
seems to agree that America is in decline.

And during that decline, we can expect to see more of what
we've already been seeing. For most people, that will mean a
"progressive" ratcheting down of quality of life, and the low-
ering of expectations.

What we won't see is some "great awakening" or a dramatic change in leadership or direction. The people who run

America aren't going to "come to their senses."

As America declines and becomes a failed or failing state, the corporations and businessmen and bureaucrats who run it will continue to preach globalism and multiculturalism and feminism.

They will continue to condemn anything that could be considered racism or tribalism—especially among whites—until they are safely in the minority. They will continue to condemn "male sexism" and continue to promote any kind of go-girl female sexism that emasculates or devalues men. They will continue to promote reverence for their own academic priest class while condemning as "extreme" any religious belief that challenges the moral authority of progressive beliefs. They will continue to promote dependence on the State for security and income and healthcare—for life itself.

And, no matter how many "conflicts" they escalate or how many people they kill or imprison or how militarized their police state thugs become, they will officially continue to condemn "violence."

They will continue to do all of this because it makes perfect sense...*for them.*

If you were the rulers and toadies of a nation in decline, whose people were bound to lose wealth and status and you wanted to protect your own interests and keep your heads, why would you *not* want to keep those people separate, emasculated, weak, dependent, faithless, fearful and "non-violent?"

Figureheads may come and go, but I see absolutely no reason why the message will change.

Many of you may see yourselves as civilized men. Sane men in an increasingly insane, vulgar and barbaric world.
But you're wrong!

YOU are the new barbarians.

The official message will continue to be that:

- If you believe that all men are not created equal

- If you believe that free men should have access to fire-arms

- If you believe the government cannot be trusted to regulate every aspect of your life

- If you believe that race means blood and heritage — not just "skin color"

- If you see that men and women are different and believe they should have different roles

- If you believe that men should act like men

- If you believe that gay pride parades and gay marriage are ridiculous

- If you believe in some "old time religion"

If you believe any or all of those things, then, according to the State and corporations, the Academia and the media, you are a *stupid, psycho, hillibilly, Neo-Nazi, woman-hating, wife-beating, homophobic throwback, reactionary Neanderthal.*

You know it. Dance to it! Make it a techno remix.
Because make no mistake: you are dangerous, traitorous and quite possibly seditious.

Well, I'm reminded of the words of rapper Eminem:

I am whatever you say I am

If I wasn't then why would I say I am

Im the paperm the news, every day I am

Radio won't even play my jam

It doesn't matter what you think you are. You are whatever they say you are. They control the message. No matter how reasonable you think your message is, *the radio is not going to play your jam.* No matter what you think you are, to them, you are the barbarians. So own it... be it. And, if you're going to be the barbarians, then start thinking like barbarians.

What does that mean? What does it mean to be a barbarian? Classically speaking, a barbarian is someone who is not of the State, of the polis. The barbarian is not properly civilized — according to the prevailing standard of the State. His ways are strange and tribal. The barbarian is an outsider, an alien.

How must a man's thinking change, when he is alienated by the State of his birth?

How does a man go from being a man of the polis to an outsider — a barbarian — in his own homeland?

These are important questions because if you see no viable political solution to the inane and inhuman trajectory of the progressive state — and I don't — then any meaningful change is going to require a lot more than collecting signatures or appealing to the public's "good sense" or electing the right candidate.

What you need is to create a fundamental change in the way that men see themselves and their relationship with the State. Don't worry about changing the state. *Change the men.* Cut the cord. And let them be born to a state of mind beyond the state.

Show them how to become barbarians and break the sway of the state. How do you do that? Well, that's something I'm going to be thinking and writing about for the next few years.

But I can offer four lines of thinking that I think could be helpful.

#1. SEPARATE "US" FROM "THEM"

This conference is about the future of identity. Which identity? Who are we talking about? Who is we? When I talk to guys about what is happening in the world right now, they're quick to tell me what we should do about it, but who is this "we?"

You and the corporations that sell you garbage food, ruin your land and outsource your jobs? You and the "expert" shills who turn your values into "psychological problems?" You and the paid-for media that mocks you? You and the Wall Street bankers who financialized the economy for their own short-term gain? You and the bureaucrats who want to disarm you and micromanage every aspect of your life? You and the politicians who open up the borders and fall all over themselves to pander to a new group of potential voters instead of working for the interests of the actual citizens of the country they swore to represent?

That "we?"

Americans, especially, are used to speaking in terms of "We the people." But there are 300 million people in the United States and that's a lot of "we." Be more specific.

Be more tribal.

One of the best pieces of writing advice I ever got was this: never say "people" when you mean "men." Well, my advice to you is to never say "we" when you mean "they" and never say "us" when you mean "them." Stop using democratic language. Stop pretending that we are all on the same team, because we're not. And we don't have to be. Decide who you really care about. Figure out what you have in common. Define your boundaries. Decide who is in and who is out. The people who are in are "us." *Those people* are "we." Everyone else this "they."

#2. STOP GETTING ANGRY BECAUSE THINGS DON'T MAKE SENSE!

Almost nothing you read or hear in the news today seems to make any sense at all.

People get so angry, so frustrated, so betrayed. It's like "our leaders" are crazy or stupid, or both. It doesn't make sense to put women in the infantry. That's obviously crazy! It doesn't make sense to encourage kids to take out college loans they'll never be able to pay back. It doesn't make sense to invite people into the country when you cannot afford to care for the people who are already here. That's nuts!

It doesn't make sense to start wars and then say you're trying to "win hearts and minds." War is not a good way to win hearts and minds! And worrying about hearts and minds is not a good way to win a war!

It doesn't make sense that bankers and CEOs get golden parachutes and go on vacation or get jobs in the administration after knowingly and intentionally destroying companies, jobs, lives, the environment — whole segments of the economy!

But if you realize that they — the people who run the country

— are doing things to benefit them and not you, everything makes perfect sense.

Consider the possibility that America's leaders really don't care if American soldiers live or die. Consider the possibility that American colleges and bankers don't care if you live the rest of your life in debt to them. They'd probably prefer it. Consider the possibility that American politicians care more about keeping their jobs in the short term and looking good in the media than they do about what happens to the people of their country in the long term. Consider the possibility that "you" are not part of an "us" that "they" care about. I promise that if you meditate upon this, things will start to make a lot more sense.

If you let go of the idea that these people are supposed to care about you or the country, and you allow yourself to see them as gangs and individuals working to further their own interests, you can relax and appreciate their crafty strategy.

Let go of foolish expectations about what these people should be doing. Step back and see them for what they are. Don't be mad. Don't be outraged. Be wise.

As Nietzsche recommended: be *carefree, mocking, and violent.*

#3. DE-UNIVERSALIZE MORALITY

Men who were raised with American, Egalitarian, "Late-Western" values want to be "good men." They want to be fair and just, and they want to be just to everyone. This can be absolutely paralyzing.

It really creates an internal conflict for men—good men—who are especially athletic or who have some kind of military or police background. They were taught and they believe in good sportsmanship and equal justice.

They want to do the "right thing," no matter what.

They want to be Batman.

However, it is also in the nature of these men—even more than other men— to think vertically, hierarchically, tribally, to think in terms of "us" and "them." To evaluate others naturally, primally, by the masculine, tactical virtues of Strength, Courage, Mastery and Honor.

But as soon as the football game or the superhero movie is over, progressive America goes back to hating and punishing those virtues. Progressive America goes back to hating and punishing men who act like men. These "good guys"... these guys who want to be heroes get blamed and played and dumped on and treated like garbage.

No matter what the progressive American message is, when it comes to men who act like men—especially white men—no one really cares if they get treated justly or fairly.

Still, these "good guys" don't want to exclude women from anything because it seems unfair they have sisters and mothers and they want everyone to have a chance. But women—as a group—don't care when men feel excluded.

In fact, when men object to anything, groups of women are the first to call them "whiners" and "losers." "Good" white guys as a group care about what happens to black people as a group. They want to make sure that blacks are being treated fairly and equally and they go out of their way to make sure they aren't "discriminating."

Do black people as a group care what happens to white people as a group?

Does a Mexican dad with three babies care whether or not some white kid from the "burbs" can get a summer landscaping job?

The problem with these late Western values is that they work best as intra-tribal values.

They only work when everyone else is connected and interdependent. Fairness and justice and good sportsmanship promote harmony within a community. But at some point, you have to draw that line. You have to decide who is part of that community and who is not.

You cannot play fair with people who don't care if you get wiped off the map. You don't have to hate everyone who isn't part of your tribe, but it is foolish to keep caring about people who don't care about you.

These heroic types are the natural guardians of any tribe,

but their heroic natures are wasted and abused when they are asked to protect everyone, even enemies and ingrates and those who despise them.

If Western Barbarians are going to hold onto any portion of their western heritage and identity, they need to resolve these moral conflicts.

They don't necessarily need to abandon morality or moral virtue, but they need to pull in their aegis and become, as in Plato's *Republic*, "noble dogs who are gentle to their familiars and the opposite to strangers."

Be morally accountable. *But only to the tribe.*

If they are going to prosper and endure in a failing nation, the New Barbarians must give up the tragic, misunderstood hero routine and realize that they aren't Batman. *Why would anyone want to be?*

#4. BECOME INDEPENDENT FROM THE STATE, AND INTERDEPENDENT BETWEEN EACH OTHER

The United States of America and its parent corporations offer a wide range of products and services. All of them have strings attached and the more you depend on them, the easier it is to control you.

It is not really much of a threat to them if you get online and "like" a naughty page or vent your lonely, impotent rage, so long as the rest of your identity folds neatly into the bourgeois American lifestyle.

So long as you still go to a make-work job at some big company and keep yourself busy for 40 or 50 or 60 hours a week so you can purchase their wide range of products and services.

And then, in the time you have left, you go online and you get to be Orthodox guy or Roman guy or Odinist guy and post cool pics of Vikings and Centurions and Crusaders.

But that's not a real identity or a real tribe or a real community. By all means, use the Progressive State and take whatever you can from it while there is still something left to take, but if you truly want some kind of "alternative lifestyle" to what the state has to offer, if you want to maintain some kind of tribal identity that can endure America's decline and collapse— also known as a sudden absence of adequate products and services—instead of "community organizing" on the Internet in your underwear or retreating to a country compound with the wife and kids, bring some of those Internet people close to you and live near each other. Take over a neighborhood or an apartment complex, start businesses and provide services that people really need.

It's great to have writers and thinkers, but you also need mechanics and plumbers and seamstresses. Serve everyone, but be loyal to people "in the family" and make them "your own."

It doesn't have to be some formal thing. Don't issue a press release. Just start quietly building a community of like-minded men and women somewhere. Anywhere.

Don't worry about creating some massive political movement or recruiting thousands or millions of people. Don't worry about changing the state. Barbarians don't worry about changing the state. That's for men of the state — who believe in and belong to the State.

Shoot for 150 people. A small, close-knit community of people working together to become less dependent on the State and more dependent on each other.

Recent immigrants—many of whom are literally "not of the State"—can serve as examples. It wasn't long ago that the Irish and Italians lived in insular communities. Think of Russian parts of town.

Look at places like Chinatown in San Francisco: every few blocks, you see these buildings marked:
Something . . . something . . . something . . . "Benevolent Association."

Sounds nice, right? Could be a front for Triad Gangs. Could be there to help Chinese schoolchildren. I have no idea. But I am sure that it is for Chinese people. There are also doctor offices and law offices and repair shops and grocery stores. There is a whole network there of people taking care of their own people first.

There is a community there of people who are exclusive, insular and interdependent. They go to each other first for what they need. They are harder to watch and harder to control. They are less dependent on the State and more dependent on each other. And when the collapse comes, they'll take care of each other first, while everyone else is waiting for the state to "do something."

Whoever your "us" is, whatever your "tribe" is, it's just an idea in your head until you have a group of truly interdependent people who share the same fate. That's what a tribe is. That's what a community is. That is the future of identity in America.

Land belongs to those who take it and hold it. And this land is no longer your land or my land — officially it's their land. You may not be able to reclaim it, at least not just right now, but you can become and live as happy Barbarians, as outsiders within, and work to build the kinds of resilient communities and networks of skilled people that can survive the collapse and preserve your identities *after the fall.*

CROM!

Men can argue forever about the details of religion.

I don't have time for any of it.

When I read arguments about interventionist gods, I see human vanity. Nothing more.

Everyone wants to believe that someone, somewhere cares about the things they do and think and feel. This is pure human vanity. The details of this or that religion are justifications that prop up this lie that makes people feel better — the comforting lie that beyond the indifference of nature and the cruelty of humanity there is a father or a family that cares about every little hope and dream and hurt. People want to believe that if they do the right things, these magic people who care about them will take their side in their petty little monkey dramas and help them when no one else will.

You don't need proof of this, because if you're reading this you are as human as I am, but for the sake of argument, look at social networking. Look at how desperate most people are to know that someone, somewhere likes their latest "status update." People want someone to care about what they did or what they hate or how something made them angry or happy or sad. We all want this in one way or another, so we take turns grooming each other like the nervous little monkeys we are.

If you pick the lice out of my hair, I'll pretend I give a shit about what happened to you at work today. Then we'll switch. That's a basic human conversation. When you're feeling lonely and there's no one else to listen, God listens. And He pretends to care.

That may be a little crass, but it's not too far from the truth most of the time. You know this, because you're human, too. Somewhere beyond pretending to care, there is actually caring, and that's what we really need from our friends and family. That's the thing we're always looking for — the emotional security of knowing we have a tribe of people who actually care what happens to us. Without a tribe, you're just a monkey standing alone on a great plain, waiting to be mauled by some beast who doesn't care about how you feel — only how good you'll taste.

Some men claim that they don't need or want any human affirmation, but they are miserable lying bastards. They can no more escape this natural human desire than they can escape a hunger for food or sexual lust. But as with lust and hunger, men can manage and control their desires and choose how to act on them, based on their idea of what is good and how they believe men should behave in the kind of human society they want.

In the modern world, our desire for affirmation is already out of control. We don't need the confidence and support of the gods. We're bombarded by reassurances and social grooming at every turn. Our human need for social affirmation has been exploited by companies who pay people to ask us how we're doing and how they can help us. Brands compete for our attention, and we're constantly polled and measured by marketers trying to figure out what pleases us or makes us laugh or makes us feel sentimental. Politicians pander to us and pretend to care what we want and whether or not we're happy. All of these people are making us feel important because they want something — every idiot knows that deep down. The affirmations are empty, but like artificial sweeteners they are close enough to the real thing to keep people coming back for more. First World men and women have come to feel entitled to this constant affirmation, and when someone fails to flatter them just because they are breathing, they become indignant and irate.

The last thing men need today is more comfort, more false affirmation. The last thing men need today is a god that cares about everything they say or do, and whether or not they've been naughty or nice.

I don't believe there is any god who cares about any man's secret feelings, or his mundane deeds.

That's why my god is CROM.

I know he's just a made-up character from the Conan stories. Since all of the other gods are just made-up stories, too, that's fine by me. Why *not* CROM?

The name CROM may come from the ancient Irish god Cromm Crúaich, who was associated with human sacrifice. Some of my distant relatives were Irish and English, and many were probably pagan Celts of some kind if you go back far enough. Some possible ancestral connection is a plus, but ultimately we know about as much about Cromm Crúaich as we know about CROM — possibly even less. All we really know about Cromm Crúaich is what we read in stories written by outsiders with their own agendas.

The same is true to a greater or lesser extent with many of the known pagan gods. I like a lot of those old pagan gods. The gods are dramatic characters that personify aspects of the human experience and nature. Their stories inspire and put some magic back into the world. I prefer the European pagan gods to the Christian god or Asian religious figures because the European pagan gods were the native gods of my ancestors, and I like their stories better, and they inspire me in a way that I want to be inspired.

But CROM is the god I need most.

CROM is the god I need because he is the opposite of the interventionist gods who care about the petty details of men's lives. You don't pray to him, because he probably won't listen, and if he hears you, he probably won't even pretend to care.

CROM is the anti-Facebook.

CROM will not "like" your spiritual status update.

There is good indication that if CROM were real, he would laugh at your "feelings" and mock your foolish "beliefs." CROM only cares about one thing, and that one thing is VALOR.

The root of the word valor indicates worthiness, and the word has come to mean the kind of worthiness made evident by the demonstration of courage in the face of danger.

What most men know about CROM comes from a speech in the movie Conan the Barbarian, when Conan attempts to pray to CROM.

> "CROM, I have never prayed to you before. I have no tongue for it. No one, not even you, will remember if we were good men or bad. Why we fought, or why we died. All that matters is that two stood against many. That's what's important! Valor pleases you, CROM... so grant me one request. Grant me revenge! And if you do not listen, then to HELL with you!"

Conan got his revenge, of course, but no one knows if CROM had anything to do with it. (And if he didn't, then to HELL with him!) Conan used CROM to put his goal into words and summon his own strength and his own courage to fight against great odds and achieve his own goal.

CROM is a god beyond good and evil. CROM is a god of self-overcoming, and self-commanding, of self-obedience and the summoning of strength in the service of will. Even if you triumph, CROM probably won't be impressed. He only cares about winners, not "survivors," and he doesn't pretend to be interested in hearing your excuses or rationalizations. Words like "fairness" and "equality" probably send him into thunderous fits of laughter.

CROM offers nothing and expects the impossible.

CROM is the god men need in a world where everyone is declared a winner just for being alive.

CROM is the symbol of the inner revolt that is necessary to push yourself through hardship even though you don't have to — even though you could just walk away.

CROM is also an exclamation.

"CROM!"

"By CROM!"

Based on the Conan stories and comics I've read, the exclamation, "CROM!" usually translates roughly to "What the fuck is this crazy new bullshit I have to deal with?!!"

If CROM is going to bother with you at all, it wouldn't be to soothe or comfort you. If CROM does anything, he's probably going make things harder. In that way, he's kind of like an older brother or ornery grandpappy who sabotages your work just to see how you'll handle it. It is not the way of CROM to offer unconditional love, it is the way of CROM to test you. CROM doesn't want to test your faith — but he will test your mettle.

From the Conan Story "Queen of the Black Coast," by Robert E. Howard, we learn this of CROM:

"…He dwells on a great mountain. What use to call on him? Little he cares if men live or die. Better to be silent than to call his attention to you; he will send you dooms, not fortune! He is grim and loveless, but at birth he breathes power to strive and slay into a man's soul. What else shall men ask of the gods?"

What else shall men ask?

What else do men need?

In an age where the gods have been driven into the shadows by the light of SCIENCE!, men must find inspiration where they can. If the old gods have become mere stories — ideas — then men are free to choose whatever story inspires them to become what they believe they should become.

I choose CROM, because he offers everything I need and nothing I don't. What I don't need any more of is already all around me.

CROM symbolizes the part of myself I need to tap into to

push myself out of the nurturing womb of false affirmation that surrounds us all, and strive out into hostile territory.

Why?

Because CROM.

THE BROTHERHOOD

"You still want to create a world before which you can kneel: that is your ultimate hope and intoxication."

— *Thus Spoke Zarathustra*

Men want to believe that they are driven by reason.

But what is reason?

Reason is not an end in itself. Reason is a way. Reason is a tool, a method of measuring options to arrive at the most desirable outcome.

How does a man choose what outcome is most desirable?

Beyond reason, there is something — a light, a perfect "form" — that must guide the use of human reason.

If you believe that the best life is for all men and women to live in absolute peace, equality and harmony, without anger, conflict or want, then you would use reason to guide your path toward that end.

If you believe, as I do, that this sort of utopian "heaven" would make men into marshmallows, and that what is best in men is the product of conflict and strife, then what seems "reasonable" or "rational" to you would be entirely different than it would be for the first person.

Likewise, when people talk about "progress," I always ask, "toward what?" Progress is only progress if it moves in a particular direction. Progress without direction is merely "movement." To move forward, you must first determine a general destination.

When men employ reason, when they are "rational," they are weighing variables in the service of some gilded idea of what is good, or right, or best. This is always a romantic idea, an impossible dream, but this impossible dream is man's ultimate hope and intoxication. Without it, no option can be "better" than another option, except when the goal is merely to "survive." And even when the only options seem to be life or death, men still have an idea of what kind of survival is no longer worth the effort. Many men will tell you that they wouldn't want to live if they lost their sight, or their legs, or their cocks. They'll say that they wouldn't want to be kept alive if they would be confined to a hospital, or attached to a ventilator, or be unable to control their bodily functions. So, even when the only goal is survival, men's choices are still guided by some emotional idea of what life is best, or better, or unacceptable.

So, if you want to know a man, and what guides his choices, his use of reason, you must understand his dream.

For most men, this dream is poorly defined. A man's dream is, after all, primarily an emotional and romantic thing. It's as emotional and romantic as ideas like "love" or "happiness," and like those words, it is usually difficult to define precisely.

As a writer, I think a lot about what I believe is best and men frequently ask me to more clearly define my position on this or that, or explain what I really want.

Of course, this perfect place, this "world that I could kneel before," is like any human home or city in that is never truly finished, and it is always, to some extent, under construction. As I learn and think, I'll continue to move things around. I will add and subtract and reposition ideas within my own hierarchy of values. If you continue to read and think, you will keep changing your idea of what is kind of life is best, too.

That is not to say that whoever learns the most or thinks the most will have the best answer for everyone. The smartest men can be incredibly stupid, sometimes almost psychopathically stupid, when it comes to conceptualizing what is best for other men. They dream the dreams that seem best to them, and as statistical outliers, their dreams sometimes have a very limited appeal to others.

I don't believe that there is a perfect society for everyone at every time in history and under every set of circumstances. For this reason, it is important to me to see different groups of people determine their own destinies. This is probably my most "universal" moral value. I don't believe that people with different interests who live far away from each other should have to agree on a way of living, and I believe that forcing them to accept a foreign or unwanted way of life is tyranny, no matter how "good" the intentions, because I believe that people should be able to determine their own idea of what is "good." I actually believe that the world is better and far more interesting if there are many cultures with different values and ideals. By that measure, I guess you could call me a multiculturalist.

So, my sacred, guiding dream is not a universal dream for everyone, but a dream of the society to which I would be most willing to surrender my precious American "individuality."

I've decided to call this dream "The Brotherhood."

The Brotherhood begins as an alliance between men against all external forces. This oath, be it formal or informal, spoken or unspoken, is the most sacred aspect of The Brotherhood. The oath of brotherhood creates a sense of "us" and establishes that "our" needs will supercede the needs of all others and outsiders. The oath creates a voluntary kinship, a sense of collective identity, a foundation of trust. The oath of brotherhood is what holds everything together, and without it, or when it has been irreparably corrupted by conniving and betrayal, The Brotherhood will inevitably fall apart.

It is precisely because this trust between men is so precarious, so fragile — especially between the leaders and followers of The Brotherhood — that it must be the most sacred of all values.

The Brotherhood must be protected and cultivated. It must be sustained and dutifully maintained, celebrated and solemnly elevated above all other things. And, in the reverence of this brotherhood, the honor — that overwhelming and ever-present concern of all men worth knowing — the honor of The Brotherhood must be elevated as well. Because men naturally evaluate each other as men according to the tactical virtues of Strength, Courage, Mastery and Honor, The Brotherhood must also maintain a culture that extols, demands and projects Strength, Courage, Mastery and Honor.

If this strikes you as unusual, it shouldn't. If you look at public architecture and statuary before 1940, even in "egalitarian" America, it is impossible to miss the monumental exaltation of strength and courage and power. Statues of the nation's great men and war heroes survey and pass judgement on us all from high stone blocks. I can walk to a park, even in Portland, stand beside a building erected by Masons and look through the trees to see a battle-ready Theodore Roosevelt mounted on a snorting bronze horse with a sword at his side. The rousing description on his plinth includes the line: "His courage stood every onslaught of savage beast and ruthless man, of loneliness, of victory, of defeat." A swaggering cult of stalwart heroes and muscular gods have defined the identity of peoples and nations across the world, and certainly across the West and in the Slavic East. The values of The Brotherhood, the values of men, the virtues that protect "us" from "them" have long been at the center of public life, at least symbolically.

The Brotherhood is the most sacred idea in my ideal society, but without family, the Brotherhood has no future. The family is the second most sacred idea. The family is a means for the continuation of The Brotherhood, and gives a sacred role to women in The Brotherhood. The ideal woman is Queen Gorgo of Sparta, proud of her role in The Brotherhood, boasting that only women of her tribe give birth to worthy men. Women are respected as women, and treated with dignity, but women know that they are not men and don't feel the need to compete with men. Men and women have separate roles, and separate social circles; they will spend time together at home but have time apart from one another to be men in the world of men and women in the world of women, as they have for most of human history. Women are not permitted to rule or take part in the political life of The Brotherhood, though women have always and will always influence their husbands. In The Brotherhood, women are trained to defend themselves and their children and their own honor, but they only take up arms as a last resort.

In very large and complex civilizations, the work of fighting is often reserved for a professional military class or caste, and "the people" put the family before The Brotherhood. I believe this is a mistake, and leads to disharmony and resentment between men.

In American society right now, for instance, the average male citizen thinks he is "too good" to fight for his people. ("What people?" is a separate discussion). He has been told that he is special and meant for "better things (like "college") and that warring is for stupid thugs who don't know any better. He may play wargames or fantasize about war, but he feels no obligation to soldiers beyond some rote display of abstract gratitude. Likewise, an unguarded discussion with American soldiers will likely reveal that even the most generous and benevolent combat-tested soldier silently or openly regards civilian men as soft, childlike, ungrateful and naive. Pick an argument with a professional soldier about his job and his disgust and disdain for the common man will rise to the surface very quickly.

It was not so long ago that Western ruling classes sent their sons to serve as military officers, or that war heroes were celebrated and elected or appointed to meaningful political positions.

Today, American elected officials are mostly from the civilian merchant class that has no meaningful relationship with the military class, and sees them only as toy soldiers to send out on violent errands of political convenience. This is divisive and destructive. In a better tribe, no matter how big or small, all men should train and be expected to defend (or aggress) as invested warriors, not mercenary "soldiers" working for paltry paychecks or to pay off college debts.

All men will not be equally able, physically, mentally or emotionally, to perform well as warriors. Some men will be better at it than others and become "lifers," and other men will do their time and then specialize in areas of work that make use of their best talents, but all men should be be initiated into

The Brotherhood. The men of a tribe should all have some connection to that role at the perimeter of society that makes all other virtue and beauty possible. No man who hasn't been part of the warrior brotherhood should have a say in governance, let alone weigh in on when to put warriors at risk. A society organized this way may be economically hobbled by the loss of a few years of study and experience in the trades or in trading, but it will be spiritually richer for the collective unity and understanding between its men.

In the triad of values for The Brotherhood, the idealized Brotherhood and its manly honor are at the top, but family and ancestry make up the two points across its base. I have never been a believer or a religious man, but ancestor worship can bridge the gap between old religion and new science. The best we can do for the dead is remember them, and every man and woman wants to be remembered. This sacred cult of remembering the dead is also what makes women so important, and makes a strong argument for the majority of men to marry — even when they are not particularly inclined to — and continue their lines. Young men should grow up knowing what their great-grandfathers and great-great-grandfathers did, and who they were, and what they believed. Their stories and jokes and skills should be passed from generation to generation. Many of our tribal ancestors didn't have writing. We do. It's shameful that we don't use it more regularly to preserve the memories of those who came before at a personal level.

This triad of The Brotherhood, The Family and The Dead are the most important features of my sacred dream, but there are certainly other values that inform what I think is good, or better.

I believe in hierarchy through meritocracy. I break here from many Radical Traditionalists enamoured with caste systems and inherited class. Many traits are heritable, but these traits are not guaranteed. I want to be ruled by great and accomplished men, not their spoiled children. I don't believe that men should inherit titles or substantial wealth. Every man should make his own way and prove his own worth.

I don't have a favorite political or economic model. I'm obviously against oligarchy and globalism, and you'll notice that my triad of social values above wasn't a stack of gold bullion. I can say that I'm tired of seeing every political thought or idea framed in terms of late 19th and early 20th Century political movements. When the Greeks and Romans used public money to build public baths, or the Vikings built a great hall, it wasn't "socialism." Every blacksmith who ever took money in exchange for his services isn't a "capitalist." And every ruler who stirred up a war or laid down some strict rules was not a "fascist." I can appreciate elements of all of these systems, and would abandon this static and contentious framework. I have called myself an anarcho-fascist (see the essay earlier in this book), but in a symbolic sense.

I believe that all rulers should have a covenant with the people, and every good leader should listen to his peers. A good ruler comes from The Brotherhood and has a responsibility to his brothers.

I'm not against some form of democratic rule, depending on what is practical for the size of the tribe. The problem with American style democracy is that leaders don't demonstrate their worth, they simply try to convince you of their worth. They feign the same interest and sincerity with every audience. They say whatever they have to say to stay in the game.

American politicians are essentially salesmen. I'm tired of being ruled by salesmen. I don't even like salesmen. I don't trust them when they start chatting me up at a store. Why would I trust them to rule me?

"Reasonable" men often say that America really needs a proven businessman to lead the country — some self-made millionaire or successful CEO. Candidates tout their business backgrounds and every so often some big-time wheeler and dealer becomes a front runner for President. Practical people seem to agree that running the nation should be like running some big company. This shows how empty the American dream is — that it seems reasonable to Americans to elect as head of state an economic leader whose greatest achievement is a lifetime spent in the shrewd service of Mammon.

I can't respect the authority of a man like that.

I believe in meritocracy, but I don't measure merit by the counting of coins.

I wouldn't mind having a king as long as he had to start at the bottom and demonstrate his worth, — and the next king did too. Give me a king who is willing to lead his men into battle on a white horse. Give me two kings, or three, but have them know that if they betray the trust of The Brotherhood, we'll stab them to death with smiles on our faces. Sic semper tyrannis.

Another key value of The Brotherhood is that "smaller is better."

I'm no fan of empires. They can accomplish great things, but at too great a social cost.

Robin Dunbar has shown that humans are limited in their ability to form deep and meaningful connections with endless numbers of people, and while large nationalist identities are possible, they generally require an outside threat or a strong source of internal coercion (propaganda combined with strict laws) to maintain for any length of time. Truly voluntaristic societies are naturally smaller.

As the scale of society grows, the stakes get higher and the rulers or administrators become less accountable to the people and more involved in their own games. Higher stakes means more corruption, or more damaging corruption. American rulers use security forces to insulate themselves from average men, and surround themselves with affirming circles of cohorts and lobbyists waving millions of dollars around, and they need these interested parties around them to help them get elected and keep their jobs. What kind of future would you expect this arrangement to produce?

I also believe that without a collective, unified identity, most men will become self-indulgent loners and soft consumers. Men are better off when they feel connected to The Brotherhood, when there is a collective sense of unity and belonging. It brings out the best in them. More men are also needed to perform tasks that give them opportunities to demonstrate the manly virtues in a smaller society. A smaller brotherhood gives more men a sense of purpose and narrative and provides more opportunities to embody the masculine virtues of The Brotherhood.

Finally, today I believe any successful Brotherhood must be *archeofuturist*.

Archeofuturism is a general approach to creating a positive vision for the future that reconciles new technology and new information with ancestral ideas about human nature and natural human lifeways. First introduced by Guillaume Faye in his book of the same name, Faye argued that while we can't go back to "the way it was" from where we are, we also can't keep pretending human nature can be erased by signing a law or a resolution or by "educating" people to become whatever we want them to become.

Modernity is too in love with the new, and tends to regard traditional human lifeways as outdated until they are somehow verified by the latest scientific study. Modern thinkers have it backwards. Scientific study should inform our understanding of human nature and potential, but it makes more sense — it is more reasonable, I think — to respect tried ways of living and tweak them according to new evidence than it is to throw out all traditional values, ideas and social institutions at once and see what happens.

Likewise, however, not all traditional ideas make sense today. As Faye suggested, we should draw a distinction between positive and harmful traditions. Many of our ancestors practiced human sacrifice to appease their gods. I think we can all agree that we don't need to start slitting throats every time crops fail just for the satisfaction of calling ourselves "Traditionalists."

To flip that coin, just because technology gives us the ability to do something doesn't mean that we should do it, or that it would be best. We are finding now, for instance, that so many industrial "innovations" in food and drug production end up making us sicker, not healthier.

And while I'm sure our ancestors would have marvelled at the possibility of making a living by sitting on their asses in climate controlled offices all day, we are finding that — like many new things that seem like a good idea at the time — this may not be the healthiest or most satisfying way to live.

Running on a treadmill is still not "better" than running on a trail, and a digital simulation of fire on a big screen TV is not as satisfying as actual fire. Porn is not better than sex. Fighting in a video game is not the same as actually fighting. A world of simulations and replacements may be "safer," but it isn't always "better."

We can and should use our understanding of evolutionary psychology, biology and the historical record to inform our perception of what kind of society we want, and stop letting sheltered academic ideologues and self-interested bureaucrats invent novel new ways to manage us as if we are ants in their own personal ant farms.

Archeofuturism is not a conservative or Traditional position, because modernity has for the most part destroyed or corrupted Traditional aspects of society to the point where there is nothing left to conserve. As Faye wrote, archeofuturism is a radical, subversive approach at this point in history.

What I've presented here isn't a comprehensive plan or even an ideology.

I'm not running for office, and I fully admit that these ideas could not be implemented in a nation the size of the United States of America, or even the State of California. But that's part of my point. Anything noble that comes from a financial empire so large grows in spite of it, not because of it.

The Brotherhood, as an aspirational ideal, is not a specific brotherhood or culture, and I am happy to support and encourage the development of many different brotherhoods that share some or all of its features — even if I would not naturally be a member of that particular tribe.

For instance, I am not a Native American, but I have been in contact with a Native American activist who read *The Way of Men* and contacted me to tell me about his brotherhood. I could never belong to that tribe, but I wish him great success in his efforts to promote virility among his tribesmen. Likewise, I am not a Christian and would never want to be part of a Christian organization, but I am pleased to see Christian men stand up for what they believe in and organize themselves in a more traditional patriarchal manner. As long as they stay out of my business and don't force me to live their way, I wish them the best.

Writing *The Way of Men* has put me in touch with members of manly tribal and nationalist organizations all around the world, and if they recognize the truth of the book's basic principles and find a way to put them into action, then so much the better — even if we end up at each other's throats!

Globalist universalism is a threat to every tribe of men. It is a threat to all of our identities and to identities yet undreamed of. It is a great eraser, a creeping consumerist "nothing" that erodes history and ancestry and the self-determination of men. Tribal brotherhood is its natural obstacle and opposite.

As a theorist of masculinity, I work in the service of brotherhoods everywhere. I work in the service of the idea of masculinity and the idea of The Brotherhood, without which masculinity is little more than a work ethic that makes men easy to manipulate. When men are asked to strive and struggle and sacrifice and prove themselves worthy, they should ask "why?," "what for?," "to whom" and "in the service of what?."

"The Brotherhood" is my best answer.

DATES OF PUBLICATION

"Violence is Golden"
Arthur's Hall of Viking Manliness (now offline), Nov 11, 2010.

"A Sky Without Eagles"
Transcript of a speech addressed to a private gathering of White Nationalists in October 2013.

"Anarcho-Fascism"
Jack-Donovan.com, March 3, 2013

"Mighty White"
Jack-Donovan.com, December 18, 2011

"Vote With Your Ass"
In Mala Fide (now offline), May 2012.

"The Grievance Table"
The Spearhead, February 4, 2010.

"There Is No Honor In Competition With Women"
The Spearhead, October 21, 2009.

"Mother May I? Masculinity"
The Spearhead, January 6, 2010.

"Draw The Line"
Jack-Donovan.com, September 23, 2012

"Everyone A Harlot"
Alternative Right, July 5, 2012.

"Train For Honor"
New to this collection.

"The Physical Challenge"
First published online at *fuckinginappropriate.com* sometime in 2012. No longer available online.

"Principles of Convenience"
Jack-Donovan.com, July 26, 2013

"The Manly Barbarian"
Counter-Currents. October 9, 2012.

"Becoming The New Barbarians"
Transcript of a speech addressed to a National Policy Institute conference held inside the Ronald Reagan Building in Washington, D.C. on October 26, 2013. The theme of the conference was "After The Fall: The Future of Identity."

"CROM"
New to this collection.

"The Brotherhood"
New to this collection.

OTHER BOOKS BY JACK DONOVAN

The Way of Men (2012)

Blood-Brotherhood &
Other Rites of Male Alliance (2010)

Androphilia (2007)

DISSONANT HUM

CASCADIA

CPSIA information can be obtained at www.ICGtesting.com
Printed in the USA
LVOW07s0751220515

439524LV00004B/220/P